Forget Me Not

A Bouquet of Stories, Thoughts
and Memories

by

Giselle Roeder

Copyright © 2015

ISBN
978-0-9949977-0-8 – (Paperback)
978-0-9949977-1-5 – (eBook)

Published by

Giselle Roeder
Nanaimo, BC, Canada V9V 1T3
www.giselleroeder.com

Also by Giselle Roeder:
"Healing with Water – Kneipp Therapy at Home "- 2000
"Sauna – The Hottest Way to Good Health" - 2001
"We Don't Talk About That" - 2014

To my grandson

Daniel Jack Roeder

Preface

The stories you are about to read are part of me and part of people who profoundly influenced me. They traveled in and out of my life in different ways. I would have loved to have shared more time with some of them. Memories of people who have long since left this planet live on in my heart.

Yes, a thousand '*Forget-me-nots*" have crossed my path. .

I would like to acknowledge the encouragement afforded to me by my fellow writers in the "Tale Spinners Club" of Parksville. I wish to thank Patricia Banks, a Nanaimo artist and writer for her input regarding the book cover; Ann Victoria Roberts, an English bestseller author, who took time out of her busy life to exchange ideas about the cover and my stories; Lyn Alexander who has written the incredible 'Schellendorf Series' set during WWI and WWII for precious advice regarding publishing; Trevor Cradduck who has spent countless hours formatting and sometimes, not so gently, pushing me to finish this book.

Each story is independent of others; some are short, some are longer. The names of individuals have been changed where necessary to protect their privacy.

Happy reading!

Giselle Roeder
Nanaimo, BC
December 2015

Table of Contents

Prologue

The airy place there on Blue Grouse
has a cedar tree behind the house.
It haunts my thoughts by day and night.
It looks so sad; too tired to fight
the plan of the builder to pull it away.
The roots are disturbed -
the surroundings bare.
There is too much sunshine
that it used to share
with other tall trees in a bygone day.
It seems to need hugging, like people do,
the loving care to make things grow,
the positive spirits, needed for health,
the balance in life for emotional wealth.
I feel with the tree -
I sense it's strain;
Should I buy the house
and try in vain
to settle the soil,
bring peace to its roots -
make home - and step out of my travel boots?
What - if the tree dies
despite my care,
who will hear my cries
when I despair?
The tree is my brother.
The tree -
is me.

I had to find my footing again in 1984. I wanted to find a place to put down roots in the city I had originally immigrated to. Twenty years earlier I had left Vancouver. Almost to the day I had come back. The roots I had grown and watered with gallons of tears in the Prairie City of Winnipeg were 'disturbed' by the people I loved most.

It's ironic but people say "Go, hug a tree" – because THIS particular tree needed care. Even after all those years I cannot forget it.

At the time I felt like a leaf blowing in the wind.

1: Charming Village Life

During my early life I thought we were quite well off or even rich. After all, there was the box with billions of Marks in a corner of our attic. We had up to four cows, a horse, several pigs, geese, ducks, chickens and lots of bunnies, pigeons, a dog and four cats.

We lived like peasants in medieval times, compared to village life today. My feelings of being 'rich' must have been triggered by the discipline our parents expected and the love and protection they provided. We never wanted for anything, except perhaps candies or cookies every day. Sweets were just for Sundays. We did not know better and accepted life the way it was. In our young years we did not know water could come out of a faucet on the wall instead of going to the pump outside. We did not know what it would be like to have constant warm water without starting a fire and heating a kettle. We did not know how food could be kept cool other than in the deep cellar under the barn. It was normal for our mother to have raw red swollen hands on wash days because of the washboard she used. We did not know there was another way to dry the laundry other than to hang it up on a clothes line outside. We did not know how to clean a carpet other than to put it over a special rod outside and hit the dust out of it with a carpet beater. The carpet beater was also used on our behind when punishment was due.

We did not know what a toilet within the house would be like. In our outhouse "things" fell into a box under the seat and, when full, it would be emptied unto the manure pile close by and covered with the dirty straw coming out of the animal's stalls. We children played tag, we played hide and seek, we skipped rope, we played hopscotch, we played ball against the house wall, we played with marbles (the glass ones were very special and were traded most carefully for several others), we played with a spinning top and we rolled and ran behind a hoop with a stick. We were kids, in the truest sense of the word. No radio, no TV, no texting, no electronics. During winter evenings our parents had more time; it was a time of storytelling, sing-alongs, card and board games. My favoured was looking at old photographs of ancestors and hearing about them.

The approximately one-thousand people in our village lived a similar life. Sunday church was a time for meeting and talking to the other villagers; the male folks would go to the pub after the service and the women would go to the cemetery and water the flowers on the graves of the dearly departed. It was their time and place to chat, and exchange the latest gossip. The big time politics in the cities did not affect this laid-back country life much. Nobody was divorced and nobody lived "in sin" or had affairs. At least, if they did, nobody knew or talked about it. We also had our "village idiot". The term is not acceptable today. We kids would run after him when he went up and down the street and repeat after him when he kicked his wooden clog way ahead: "Otto – Puff! Otto - Puff". We went everywhere on our own, to the school, to the beach and even to the city two kilometers away. Sadly all those simple childrens' activities have no place in today's society anymore. Kids nowadays don't know how to be real kids anymore.

We were happy, had no behavioral problems and if we did slip we got the punishment which we accepted as deserved and normal. I dare say all the village families were happy, just like we were. Life was simple as one day followed the other.

2: Granny and her Fairy Tales

The children agreed their paternal grandmother was the most beautiful woman they knew. She was the most important person sharing their daily life until the war tore them apart. She was the one telling them all the wonderful fairy tales during twilight hours, sitting around the old fashioned tiled warm oven in a corner of her living room, their daddy's cat Peter between them. They asked:

"Why is Hänsel and Gretel's stepmother so bad? And why is Snow-White's mother so mean?"

Their mother never had much time for them. There was so much work on the small farm with a horse, a couple of cows, several pigs, lots of geese, ducks and chickens and a new baby every two or three years. Therefore it was Granny who explained why those stepmothers did what they did.

"Hänsel and Gretel's father did not earn enough money for her to buy food. The children were starving. There was never enough to eat for all of them. She was just at the end of her wits. She might have sat in a dark corner and cried when the children were gone. People do things they wouldn't do if they are pushed too hard and see no way out. And the other, Snow-White's mother was so terribly vain she couldn't stand it when someone else was prettier, even if it was her own daughter. Better learn to accept others the way they are, pretty or not."

Granny further explained that, "When a father and his children have lost their mom they really need a new one to take care of the family and the housekeeping. There is cooking and washing and cleaning and much more you'll never see. Their dad still needs to go to work and earn money to support his family. If he was lucky and found a new mommy they could still be a family. Otherwise the children might be placed in an orphanage or sent away to strangers. You see, stepmothers are very important." Granny would take a deep breath and shake her head:

"I don't understand why stepmothers in many fairy tales are made to look so bad. It's not fair. I believe these are brave women who take on a father and his little ones. Often the children make her life very difficult because they want their old mommy back, even if she is in heaven. They might feel it is the new mom's fault their real mom is not around anymore. No, I don't envy these women at all, no matter what. It is a great responsibility and lots of hard work to help raise someone else's children."

But when she told a story about a baby born who needed two new parents and explained why it needed to be adopted, the children were quite upset about such a possibility.

"Granny, why would any mother not want to keep her baby? She didn't die, did she?"

Through her stories this granny made it easy for her grandchildren to understand why some mothers are just too young to be mommies, or they don't even have a daddy for the baby to take care of both of them. Granny made up lots of the fairy tales or altered them to prepare her grandchildren for the troubles and challenges life can bring.

"Remember, when your mother had put duck eggs under a mother hen to breed? Remember what happened? The hen took care of the little ducklings after they hatched. They cuddled under her for warmth and mother hen even tried to teach them the way of chickens, she didn't realize they were not chicklets. The little ducklings ran after her wherever she went. She was their mother in every way that counts. Remember the story about the wolf that raised an abandoned baby? Or the monkeys who raised the boy Tarzan and he thought he was a monkey? And how it troubled him that his body wasn't covered with hair?"

These stories left a big impression on the young minds. They would run to their granny and ask if they were stepchildren or adopted when their mother was cross with them. It troubled Emma, the oldest child, the most and she suffered her whole life because she was always thinking about it. In her head she kept playing out scenarios with "what if…"

Yes, this grandmother was very special. She always knew the simple answers to every question. Was it because she went to church every Sunday? Her praying hands left an indelible imprint in the soul of Emma, who was a deep thinker and seemed to be very spiritual. She often thought she saw ghosts behind people, their guardians. Emma always listened very carefully and never forgot a word she heard. Fairy tale or not, she took everything for real. Many of the stories her granny told caused her bad dreams.

Granny had grown up speaking mainly Low German like most people in the small village. She often had trouble pronouncing some words in High German. The parents wanted to prepare their children for a better education speaking only High German. It wasn't easy for Granny to please her son, their father. Emma once listened to an exchange between her and her dad. Granny was knitting and her dad was reading the newspaper. Suddenly he put it down and looked at his mother:

"Mother, - it is not 'Gesus', - it is 'Jesus'."

"Son, what are you talking about? You told me to speak High German to the children, and then the 'j' in Jesus is pronounced 'g' like in 'go' and not as it would be in Low German 'jo'."

"You are right Mother, but 'Jesus' is a name and it needs to be pronounced with a 'j' like in Joseph, the way it is written and not 'Gesus'. You wouldn't say 'Gohanna' to Johanna, would you?"

"Oh… Gosh, surely not. I never thought of that. No son, you know I wouldn't. I always thought, I don't know, I always thought Jesus was just called Jesus for some reason but I never thought it was his name. Why did people call him Jesus and not by his family name? He did have parents, Mary and Joseph. What was their family name? Did Joseph not give him his name because he was not his, but God's son? Was Christ his second name? He would need a name to be registered, wouldn't he? After all, they were on their way to be registered when the child was born in Bethlehem. I am puzzled, son. I have thought about all of this quite a bit. I could but I don't want to ask the pastor about it. He would just tell me he was Jesus Christ and it is what it is and I shouldn't question it. His answers about other bible stories are the same. I am trying to understand, son, I really do. I think I understand but maybe I don't understand completely. At least now I'll remember not to speak to the children of 'Gesus' anymore."

"No Mother, - not of 'Gesus' but there is no problem telling them all about Jesus. You know Mother, there is a two-thousand year old history connected to it and it's not just a religious or church matter. I believe this particular history is also a big part of education. The children need to learn all there is to learn and I am very proud of you helping me to the best of your ability. You are doing alright, Mother. Please forgive me if I offended you. I only tried to help when I corrected you. I mean well."

"I know that, my boy."

It was hard for Emma to understand why Grandma called her father "my boy." Granny was such a small woman and he was such a big strong man and all the people in the village respected him a lot. She didn't think for one minute anybody would have thought of him as a boy. It was hard to think he had been a boy at one time, even a baby before that. Emma decided:

"I like him better the way he is now. When I grow up I'll marry him."

3: Horses – and their Shoes

Would children nowadays have a chance to see how a horse gets new shoes? Do they have a chance to hear the "swish" when the blacksmith places the new horse shoe into cold water for a second or two before he places and fits it onto the horse's hooves? Would they ever have a chance to experience the special "smell" when the red-hot iron horseshoe is fitted onto the horse's hooves? Can they ever see how the leg to be fitted is lifted by another man, usually by an apprentice? Would they feel pain inside themselves like I did, seeing those huge nails driven into the hoof to hold the iron? Would they even know what a farrier is? Hardly.

I remember it all so well. I know about the 'swish'. I remember what it smelled like. I remember being afraid the horse would be hurt. How can the glowing iron not hurt? And what about the long nails with the almost square head that go into the horseshoe to hold it in place? How can the horse stand it? I didn't realize when I was a child that the bottom of the horse's hooves are something like a very thick callous, compared to a very thick toe or fingernail of ours without nerve endings in it. Once I saw a horse bucking while watching and I was afraid my dad would get hurt. He was kicked and fell over but he was quick to get up and went on with his job. He explained to me later it was the first time this young horse got 'shoes' so naturally it was frightened.

I wonder how and where the race horses are shoed or the horses belonging to hobby riders. There still must be 'farriers' around, we just don't know about them. Maybe school children would love to have excursions to see it for themselves.

4: Magic Hands

Many children had the measles and I got them too. My eyes hurt and I was very sick. I felt lousy, alone and sad, forgotten by everyone. The room was dark with the shutters closed. As the sunlight came through the slanted openings, I imagined it as long, silent fingers playing with the bits of silver and specks of brown in the dark blue wallpaper. I imagined faces in the shadows caused by the lilac trees outside – here and there a ship, and there was the good Lord himself on a cloud with some angels around Him. He had friendly, old eyes but He wiggled a finger at me attached to a long, sinewy hand. I was not afraid but just kept on looking. The hand was white with a touch of pink and I could almost see through it. It was a beautiful hand.

The hand was cool and soft. I felt it on my forehead. It helped my eyes not to hurt so much but I did not want to open them. I wanted to feel those cool fingers. Was I an angel now, like those behind Him? It did not matter. I felt suspended between being and not being, I was floating. Please God, just a little longer...

Was it this plea or was it the voice coming from a distance: "She has quite a high temperature and she is delirious..."

All of a sudden, I was back in my bed, the perspiration trickling into my ears. They hurt too. The long fingers and the streaks of sunlight were gone. There were no faces, no ships, no God, no angels on the wall, just the dark blue wallpaper with bits of silver and specks of brown. This used to be my father's room. My bed was a black ebony sleigh bed. My father had told me proudly it had been his before he got married.

I opened my eyes just a bit and looked right into Granny's wrinkled face. Her one hand was on my forehead and she took one of my hands into her other one.

"Did you have a nice dream, my girl? You smiled and you looked so happy."

I just nodded. I didn't want her to laugh at me if I told her of the things I had seen. She belonged to my sister Christel. She always hugged Christel, cuddled her, held her on her lap, stroked her wavy hair, and comforted her when she was crying. I was allowed to sit beside her, close enough, but never on her lap. She never stroked my hair.

Tears were stinging my eyes. I closed them again. Granny's hand felt so good on my forehead and I wished she would not take it away. I thought of how beautiful her hands were, even though they were wrinkly or perhaps maybe because they were wrinkly. Her face was beautiful and wrinkly too. Often, when I looked at her, I wanted her to hug me so badly it hurt. My mother did not hug me either, nor did my father. There was just a handshake and a light formal, "Good Night" kiss on the cheek – nothing else. But I could not let anybody know or show how much I wanted to hug or be hugged – only babies did that. I was a big kid now, a kid ready to go to school. Maybe it was good to be sick. I could feel the hand on my head and it felt good. I did not want it to stop.

"I want to look like Granny when I am a grandmother".

My ears got worse and Dad had to pick up the doctor from the city. Lucky he had a motorbike. Granny had to put special drops into my ears at frequent intervals. The drops felt cool and tickled as they ran down into my ear canal. I asked where Mom was. Granny explained she was not allowed to come close to me because I was contagious. Mom had never had the measles and when grownups get them, they could die. The measles were also

14

dangerous for a new baby. Which new baby I thought, but was too tired to ask.

"Don't worry. Your mother often stands at the door and looks at you. She hopes you will get well soon."

During my whole childhood, I had recurring ear infections. My ears are still very sensitive. Noise hurts, even drives me to tears. I cannot stand windy days without a cover. I now take ear plugs to concerts. Can you imagine falling asleep when it is too loud? It seems nature has a way of helping itself. I have fallen asleep several times. Do the hearing cells get damaged anyway?

5: Winnie the Pooh

One hundred years ago on August 24th 1914 Lt. H. Colebourn, a veterinarian with the Royal Canadian Army Veterinary Corps bought an orphaned female bear cub from a hunter who had killed her mother. Having lived in and loved Winnipeg he named her "Winnipeg Bear". The little bear became his companion on his way to England where he was to train for fighting in WWI. The bear became the army mascot and during rest time played with the soldiers. Its name was shortened from "Winnipeg Bear" to just "Winnie". Winnie lived out her life in the London Zoo where she was a star attraction. She died a natural death in 1934.

Winnie was the inspiration for one of the best loved children's books of all time. When the author, A.A. Milne read the story to his son the youngster called her 'Winnie the Pooh' and also named his teddy bear after her. Stories about 'Winnie the Pooh' have inspired generations of children and they still do. The children in England vote it their most favorite book, year by year, by year!

A "Winnie the Pooh Gallery" with memorabilia collected by the Assiniboine Zoo in Winnipeg is an attraction not only for children but adults alike. Another author, Ms. Appleby has written a biography of 'Winnie the Pooh' and her Winnipeg connection.

Say "Hi" to the bronze statue of Lt. Colebourn and 'Winnie' in the Assiniboine Zoo's Nature Playground - next time you visit Winnipeg, Canada.

6: Pineapples and Spaghetti Grow on Trees?

No, they don't. I have had people asking me if pineapples grow above or below ground! A good question. Many years ago the BBC in England managed to fool some people into believing in spaghetti trees. The pineapple plant is actually related to the 'Bromeliad' - a plant we buy because it has such a beautiful long lasting flower in the centre. It's hard to imagine how pineapples grow if you hold one of these spiky ripe fruits in your hand. The pineapple is a plant like a bromeliad with spiky hard leaves, can grow a meter wide and a metre high with a flower in the centre out of which will grow a stem with the developing fruit. The crown of the fruit, again with spiky leaves, can be removed with a slight twist and pull and used to prepare for planting outdoors or even in a pot indoors. It will not grow as big, wide and tall indoors as it does outdoors under the right conditions.

A pineapple is the fruit of a blooming flower. I have never seen one in bloom but certainly eaten a few hundred of this delicate fruit. I cringe when I see people cutting out the inner slightly harder stem. This stem is the central feeding tube for the fruit. It contains everything the fruit needs to grow, ripen and develop the delicate unique flavour. It is full of enzymes and vitamins and certainly contains more of these than the fruit itself. Therefore, always eat the stem as well. In commercial harvesting the stem is removed for its high content of "Bromelain", a protein digesting enzyme. You are familiar with the canned pineapple rings, right? These may be refreshing but they have lost most of their nutritious value. Eaten fresh and ripe you get most of your daily requirement of vitamin C, a good variety of the B vitamins, a lot of essential minerals and the special enzymes bromelain and papain, another protein digesting enzyme. Eat fresh pineapple

19

after a heavy meal! Native people of certain countries cut up the stem, marinate it and use it for tenderizing meat. Folk medicine recommends pineapples for arthritis and the prevention of other diseases. I am certain your grandma has told you more than once "An apple a day keeps the doctor away." I believe a variety of fruit will do so as well, including the "pine-apple".

Once the pineapple is cut off from its mother plant it will not grow or ripen anymore. Before you buy it in a store, check if it is ripe: Pull on the small centred leaves of the crown. If they come out easily, it's ripe. Also, try a little twist of the whole crown and if you feel it is moving easily, it is ready. Smell it at the bottom, it should give you a fresh and not yet fermenting whiff of its scent.

Eat it as fresh as possible. Use it in stirfry AFTER cooking, in deserts, on cakes or on its own. I love adding it to baby pork ribs once they are done. Cooking destroys the enzymes. If you would like to grow a pineapple plant, save the crown you twisted off. Pull out all the small and some of the larger leaves at the bottom and cut the base into an inverted pyramid. Some people advise placing it above water until the first roots appear. Others say "not necessary, just plant it into a pot and place mulch around it". Apparently it is very easy to grow indoors but it takes about two years until a flower and then the fruit appears. It likes sunshine but also does alright in dappled shade. Frost will kill it. Watch out for little suckers, you can plant those as well. The pineapple plant hardly needs any water. Just keep a little around the leaves the same way you care for your bromeliad. The lowest rotting leaves feed the plant. It's nature's fertilizer.

As for spaghetti trees – wait for April Fools' Day.

7: WWI – 100 Years Since and Counting...

A shot was fired, followed by another. Those shots killed two people, one of them the heir apparent to the Habsburg throne: Franz Ferdinand, Archduke of Austria, the other his wife. The Archduke Franz Ferdinand had married his wife Sophie, a Czech-born countess for love. Her bloodline was not good enough for the aristocratic houses of Europe. Before they were married, the treatment of his beloved caused Franz Ferdinand to be antagonistic towards the Slavic countries.

Actually the shots killing both of them were the second assassination attempt on the same day, June 28th 1914. After the official part of the day the couple was on route to the hospital to visit the wounded from the earlier unsuccessful bomb attack. The driver made a wrong turn and when someone alerted him he stopped right in front of the Serb assassin Gavrilo Princip. He fired those two fatal shots from just four feet away.

In history class we learned the shooting of the Archduke Franz Ferdinand in Sarajevo started WWI. Did the shooting really start WWI? Yes and no. It certainly hastened it, but the plans which would lead up to WWI had already been drawn up some ten years earlier. The Schlieffen plan, updated and modernized by Moltke was the 'fore-runner' so to-speak, with an eye on how Germany could defeat France and Russia.

This first shooting set off a lot of uncountable other shots: Millions of men were killed in a war supposed to end all wars. It is known as "The Great War". Not so much because it was 'great' but for the fact it involved the whole world. Expected to last only a few weeks or maybe a few months, it lasted four years and the outcome was one nobody could have expected:

- the end of the Empire of the Habsburgs,

- the abdication of the German Emperor,
- the end of the Czar-ruled Russia,
- the rise of socialism, communism and, last, but not least,
- Nazism and the rise of Adolf Hitler and his aim for a "Thousand-Year-Reich".

Those first two shots changed the world.

History writers still argue about the real reason for WWI – but every single one is just speculating. We will never know. Those first shots were the "starter's pistol" shot for the war but the true reasons had been smouldering for years. Many books have been written on WWI and writers today are still trying to dig deeper. One of the most frequent questions in discussions is the fact the Archduke had not been protected at all. It raises the question: "Was the plot planned? Was he supposed to be killed? Who was behind it all? What was the real reason?"

We will never know. Maybe the WWI General Ludendorff was right when he told Hitler: "Peace is just an interlude between wars." Did the years between WWI and WWII prove his theory? We have enjoyed a long period of peace in our part of the world but if we look at the horrors of war in the Middle East and the ongoing strife in other areas – I for one shake in my boots. Having lived through and survived WWII, I would not like to see yet another world war with a number III attached to it.

8: Start of World War II

Dinner in Pomerania was eaten at what we would call lunch time: between 12.00 noon and 1.00 PM.

The blacksmith put his hammer down and took the big heavy leather apron off. The cobbler pushed his stool aside and left his work to be continued later. The farmer came home from the fields and took care of the horses before he entered the kitchen. Each of their women had prepared a hearty meal. Sitting around the table the children were told they should be seen but not heard. It mostly went for the women as well. The men had discussed the possibility of war for the last few days.

I was just over five years old and a real 'father's girl', hanging on every one of his words with big eyes and an admiring, curious mind. He employed several men in the smithy, a couple of them young apprentices. They would all sit around the large table in our country kitchen where our meals were taken and talk. And talking they did! There was no chance for it in the work room when the fires were blazing and crackling, the hammers striking the red-hot iron on the anvils. When shaped into parts for machinery or horse shoes with sparks flying and then dipped into cold water, the hissing sound would add to the cacophony of noise. I loved standing in the big open door and watching it all, wondering why their hair did not catch fire.

On September 1st, 1939 their talk was subdued and serious with the palpable underlying fear of being conscripted into the army. War was imminent. The German army had entered Poland. The radio announced later that war had been declared. It was a very sad day in our village. People stood together in groups and I was holding on to my father's hand. All the people looked and sounded as if someone had died and they had all come from a funeral.

The rest is history. September 1st 2014 was the 75th anniversary of that sad day long ago. I remember it so well. In 2014 the Polish leader, Donald Tusk, laid a wreath at the memorial of the fallen young soldiers in Gdansk and warned:

"This is no time for beautiful speeches or naïve optimism looking at the conflict between the Ukrainian troops and the pro-Russian forces."

Did I hear the far sound of bells ringing for WW III?

Now it's just a year later and millions of Syrians have left their country. Where are those people to go? When I grew up Christmas 1944 was the last year of my childhood. I did not know it then. I was only eleven years old in 1945 when millions of us were evicted by Russia and Poland from our homes. So I know what it's like. But we were Germans being pushed across the Oder River to another part of Germany, the same country with the same language. Our homeland was ceded to Poland. We had no chance to ever go back. Years later, when some sort of political 'order' was restored after the total ruin WWII had foisted on most of the big cities, many people had not been able to put down new roots. They were not even well liked by their own countrymen, looked down upon and considered second class citizen. They had nothing more to lose as they had lost everything already. Many applied for emigration to other countries once it was possible, mostly to the American Continent, USA and Canada.

Right now we are experiencing this new wave of refugees who are not evicted but escape out of fear and desperation and of their own free will to find another country where they hope to start a new life, safe from war and strife. Civil war in their homeland hardly leaves them any choice. Most of them want to go to Germany since this country has opened its borders and hearts to take in hundreds of thousands. Austria has accepted as many as they could, Hungary has built a wall at their border to keep them out. Many countries are simply overwhelmed and have no means to accept and care for more. Sadly, Syrian refugees aren't the only ones according to media reports. People from several other countries in the Middle East and North Africa add thousands to the numbers. Several millions are now seeking a place to live plus hundreds of thousands live in tent cities in neighbouring countries. Watching the television videos brings to mind that we, in 2015, are witnessing the greatest migration of people since the second century A.D. with a peak during the fifth and sixth and right up to the eleventh century. Compared to the medieval times it now happens in the reverse direction.

If these resettlements go well and without another war what will the world map look like in another generation, two or three? I leave you to your own thoughts. There are no easy answers. Maybe there aren't any answers at all.

9: VE Day – May 8th, 1945

Cause for Celebration?

Yes, for "Victory" in Europe the allied forces had cause to celebrate. It was a victory for the allies but for all Germans living in the eastern part of Germany, taken and occupied by the Russian forces, this was no time for celebration. We were starved and both physically and emotionally exhausted. We functioned like automatons from day to day. The Daily Mail in Britain declared "It's All Over" but was it really?

One cannot help but be reminded of a quote from Charles Dickens' "A Tale of Two Cities":

"It was the best of times, it was the worst of times, it was the age of wisdom, it was the age of foolishness, it was the epoch of belief, it was the epoch of incredulity".

It was definitely the worst of times for all of us evicted from our homes in East Prussia, Silesia and Pomerania. We were forced to trek with hundreds of thousands of other displaced persons on the road to nowhere, next to the Russian war machinery. It happened a few weeks AFTER the war had been officially over. We didn't know the war was over and certainly had no cause for celebration. We were hungry, had no change of clothing and no shoes, slept in barns at the best of times and under the stars or under overhangs of buildings. I am not sure it could be regarded as an age of wisdom either, but it did mark an epoch of incredulity. With no journalists, media like radio or newspapers in Germany the suffering and plight of ordinary German citizens was never reported. Ask any older German person now and they will tell you "we don't talk about that."

10: Churchill's Incredible Foresight

It was on March 5th 1946, almost a hundred years ago, just one year after the WWII victory of the Allied troops. Winston Churchill who had failed re-election as Prime Minister of Britain was invited to give a speech at Westminster College in the small city of Fulton, Missouri in the USA. Churchill titled his talk "The Sinew of Peace". Winston Churchill was accompanied by President Harry S. Truman to Fulton, population 7000. However, the crowd who came to hear the speech numbered 40.000, and it became famous as the "Iron Curtain Speech".

Churchill pointed out he was not speaking as a politician or a statesman, but as a private person: "I am only expressing my personal thoughts and opinions". Before the speech the US and Britain had been concerned about their post-war economy and were extremely appreciative of the proactive role the Soviet Union had played in ending WWII. This speech changed the view with which the democratic West viewed the communist East.

I quote from this speech:

"From Stettin in the Baltic to Trieste in the Adriatic, an 'Iron Curtain' has descended across the continent, the division of Europe into east and west. Behind that line lie all the capitals of the ancient states of Central and Eastern Europe. Warsaw, Vienna, Berlin, Prague, Budapest, Belgrade, Bucharest and Sofia; all these famous cities and the populations around them lie in what I must call the Soviet sphere, and all are subject, in one form or another, not only to Soviet influence but to a very high and in some cases increasing measure of control from Moscow. The Russian-dominated Polish Government has been encouraged to make enormous and wrongful inroads upon Germany, and

mass expulsions of millions of Germans on a scale grievous and undreamed of are now taking place. The Communist parties, which were very small in all these Eastern States of Europe, have been raised to pre-eminence and power far beyond their numbers and are seeking everywhere to obtain totalitarian control."

Let me intersperse a personal note here. My family was just one of the millions evicted and on the road to nowhere next to the Russian war machinery on their way to conquer Berlin in 1945. Later I was just one of the people required to join the Communist Party or else…I was just one of the hundreds of thousands who escaped before the Berlin Wall was built to keep the inhabitants from leaving the country. Thinking back it is unbelievable how it was possible for people to live like that. How was it possible that many became faithful loyal communists? It was a new generation. How could the boys we grew up with, who were cousins, friends or schoolmates, be able to shoot at you if you were trying to escape? Reading the full content of Churchill's speech I can't help but admire the man for his foresight. It is incredible to think he was speaking to 40.000 people, about, as he put it, his private thoughts, in a small American city which had not endured any of the wartime atrocities committed by all sides.

It is believed this speech was the beginning of the Cold War. Churchill went on to explain the close connection the UK had with Russia over many years before and following WWI and briefly mentioned his wartime 'comrade' Marshal Stalin. He pointed out that the US was standing on the pinnacle of world power together with the responsibilities, and the anxiety to go with it. Not even a year after WWII he envisioned another war if precautions were not taken seriously and soon.

Quote:

"When I stand here this quiet afternoon I shudder to visualise what is actually happening to millions now and what is going to

happen in this period when famine stalks the earth. None can compute what has been called 'the un-estimated sum of human pain.' Our supreme task and duty is to guard the homes of the common people from the horrors and miseries of another war. We are all agreed on that."

Churchill talked about the UN, the successor of the League of Nations. He pointed out the strong and the weak spots. He, in 1946 envisioned an army made up of all member nations but was against giving them all the power especially not the secrets connected with the atomic bomb. He even foresaw the army from every country involved wearing the same uniform with just different badges. They should be trained in their own country but moved around under the power of the organisation, however, they should never be required to move against their own country. Churchill stated he had had this vision already after WWI.

He went on to speak about police states, dictatorships, people living without rights, free elections, or without fear. But Churchill also pointed out

"We have no right to interfere in countries we haven't conquered in war, - but we must never cease to proclaim in fearless tones the great principles of freedom and the rights of men which are the joint inheritance of the English-speaking world and which through Magna Carta, the Bill of Rights, the Habeas Corpus, trial by jury, and the English common law find their most famous expression in the American Declaration of Independence."

He talked of hunger, starvation and deprivation which had not yet been overcome by March 5th 1946. He quoted an old friend of his, Mr. Bourke Cockran, an actor, who had told him *"There is enough for all. The earth is a generous mother; she will provide in plentiful abundance food for all her children if they will but cultivate her soil in justice and in peace."* Churchill

31

foresaw an unprecedented age of plenty coming. Looking back over the last sixty years he was right. Never have people lived so well. He went on to extoll the need to adhere to the principles of the United Nations to prevent another war. He said *"I do not believe Russia desires another war, what they desire is to enjoy the fruits of the war and the expansion of their power and doctrines."*

I would like to finish the excerpt of Churchill's famous speech with these words of his:

"Last time I saw it all coming and cried aloud to my own fellow-countrymen and to the world, but no one paid any attention. Up till the year 1933 or even 1935, Germany might have been saved from the awful fate which has overtaken her and we might all have been spared the miseries Hitler let loose upon mankind. There never was a war in all history easier to prevent by timely action than the one which has just desolated such great areas of the globe. It could have been prevented in my belief without the firing of a single shot, and Germany might be powerful, prosperous and honoured today; but no one would listen and one by one we were all sucked into the awful whirlpool. We surely must not let that happen again."

And to think he said all this in 1946!

My question to you today: Where is the "Iron Curtain" Churchill talked about now? Do we still have an iron curtain? Do Winston Churchill's statements from March 1946 have value today? What would this far-thinking man say to us if we could listen to him now, about seventy years after his famous speech? Who is it who is whispering behind an 'Iron Curtain' now? And where is it if it exists? And who is in control of it? Opening or closing it?

11: Dutch Clogs and a Nazi Flag Dress

Several years after WWII ended life had, ever so slowly, returned back to a bit more normal and I had become a teenager. We lived in the eastern sector of Germany, in 1945 and 1946 a country without shops of any kind. I had outgrown the clothing my mother had made from rags and "one dress out of two", donations from relatives or neighbours. Would it ever have been nice if jeans had been invented already! All the kids would have looked more alike. There would not have been so much heartbreak with the teasing and bullying for the weird clothing my sisters and I had to wear going to school. I will never forget the three winters when I wore an old torn black form-fitted ladies coat with green patches and a huge big bust line, stuffed with horse hair. I was only eleven, starved and thin as a stick. There was no choice: I was lucky to have found the coat under a bush where someone had discarded it. At least I had a coat during the winters 1945, 1946 and 1947. My uncle Fritz did a deal by trading fish he had caught for some Dutch clogs. Those wooden shoes kept my feet very warm. But imagine the picture:

A small, starved thin eleven year old kid with a big-busted fitted ladies coat and Dutch clogs! I wish I had a photograph. Today I can smile about it but back then it caused me many tears. I refused to go to high school. I had nothing to wear. The teasing was already bad enough in the small village where we lived, but going to a city school? I'd have died…

I got a chance to learn how to sew but I had to bring my own material. You couldn't buy anything. A kind neighbour gave me a big Nazi flag she had unearthed in an old trunk in her attic. Her family and mine would have been arrested if anybody would ever have found out. To own a Nazi flag was a criminal offence after

WWII in the Russian sector. I undid all the seams, took the white center and the black stitched on swastika apart and my seamstress teacher helped me to design a pretty "country dress".

The body of the dress was fashioned out of the red material with a wide swinging skirt, a white insert around the neck with small strips out of the black swastika around the skirt and the insert and a black belt. It wasn't quite Bavarian style, but very similar, albeit with no apron. It was a fun dress and I happily wore it until I grew out of it and passed it on to my third sister Ingrid. I wonder whatever happened to it after Ingrid died.

12: Work in an Office?

"Have you ever thought of learning to type and work in an office?" The question came out of the blue.

We were re-planting strawberries in one of my father's garden. Over the winter they had made so many new plants, reaching out with those long tendrils. My dream was to become a gardener. It was just four years after WWII ended. We lived in East Germany where it was impossible to get an apprenticeship in any trade. Trade Schools were not in existence either. Work in an office? My hands stopped working and I stared at Dad. He told me about this elderly couple he had met who taught typing and shorthand.

"If you take the three months' course I'll pay for it."

I jumped at the chance. It started on the first of June 1949. My sewing class was long finished and I had some reasonably nice clothing. You won't believe it, but I loved the dress I made out of an old Nazi flag. And another out of my mother's old grey spring coat. My aunt had also given me several moth-ball smelling ancient dresses and it was the in-thing to make one out of two. We had also received three care packages from the USA with several used dresses but mainly milk powder, rice and other food items which wouldn't go bad. By taking typing and steno I wouldn't have to crawl over the farmer's fields again to thin out turnips or plant potatoes like I did during summers of the last few years.

Eight students shared ONE typewriter! How could we ever learn you ask?

Imagine this:

We had to find a piece of cardboard. That, in itself, was a difficult task but the neighbour who had given me the Nazi flag for my dress also donated a box she found in her attic. Made into several different pieces I could even help some of the other students. Cut to size, the letters of the key board were copied onto it. On this piece of card board we had to learn the position of the letters and do the typing exercises so our fingers would find the required letters.

Don't laugh - it was just the way it was when I was a teenager. After two weeks we weren't allowed to look at our "keyboard" anymore. A second piece of cardboard was hung around our neck to hide what our fingers were doing. The nice

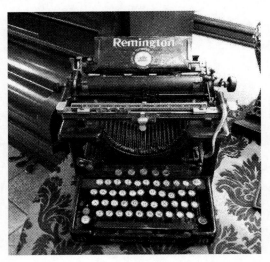

old couple would dictate something and our fingers had to "type" the letters. They always saw when someone lifted the wrong finger. I "typed" on this cardboard for hours at home. My mother would tease me endlessly but I was determined to be 'the best' of the class. It was great fun when we

finally had turns on the real typewriter.

For you this may be hard to believe with all the gimmicks you have. Computers and i-Pads and what-have-you… And before you ask, - no, we did not know anything about electric typewriters. If my memory serves me right, I could type 126 words (or letters?) per minute and in shorthand I could do about a hundred or was it two-hundred? It's so long ago. Yes, I had done well in my shorthand/typing course. I found it intriguing to be able to make those little scribbles and read them. Amazing how fast one could write. I loved it! I asked my father to dictate or read to me and I would write it. He couldn't believe I was able to read it back to him, even hours later or the next day. He was proud of me. He thought my next course should be book-keeping and it was. It was called "double bookkeeping." Was I ready to start working in an office? I thought I was. Finding a job was the greatest problem.

On weekends I worked as a waitress in a terraced garden restaurant when the weather was good. I was happy and super nice to the people in my section. I smiled and told them of the best things on the simple menu. I talked to them as if they were my best friends. I ran up and down those terraces all day and was exhausted by sundown. My guests complimented me and always wanted to sit in my area when they came back a second time. They tipped extra well. After work I had to turn all the money including tips over to the owner. Mrs. Porter would check my order vouchers and take the money owed to the restaurant. Almost daily she would take more than I owed her and excused her actions with, "Nobody gives such high tips. You must have made a mistake and not turned in your order vouchers. I only allow six Marks in tips for each day."

She would keep what was rightly my money. As a matter of fact, I would not get ANY food out of the kitchen without the numbered voucher. After this happened a few times and I was accused of stealing, I was very upset and mentioned it to my father. He got angry and told me sternly, "You tell her you quit." So I did.

Through my father I had an interview with the ship wharf's inventory office. The trouble was, I still looked like a kid with my braids wound around my head. Dad did not allow me to have my hair cut short and it was not common to wear it open as the girls do now. The pony tail was not "invented" yet or at least had not made it across the border from West to East Germany. I begged to have it cut or get a perm but Dad thought then I would look like a floozy because I still had a kid's body. Nevertheless, to my surprise the interview went well and I was hired with a six week probation period in November 1949.

It was a smelly, messy, dark industrial office. I worked with another woman. It was not office work the way I had envisioned it. I did not like the job but I had made up my mind: I needed experience and this was just a stepping stone. I was determined to work my way up. The first few days I had to count different types of nails, screws and nuts and mark down the few other items on the shelves in a printed inventory list. Products were scarce. The men were often sitting around and do nothing because the items they needed for repairs or production were not available. They were smoking, telling coarse jokes, laughing and flirting with the woman who was my supervisor. They got paid anyway. It wasn't their fault they didn't have what they needed to do their jobs. The political system in East Germany was such that it offered every able man and woman a job. There was absolutely no unemployment. As long as you turned up at the job site, even if you did nothing, you got paid.

My work office was in disarray and the woman in charge did not let me get it cleaned up or organized the way I thought it should or could be. She did what little letter typing there was. When she had nothing to do she was reading a book or filing her nails.

Once a month we got a form consisting of a number of pages. Every page, also the back side, had rows of questions on it. It was an order form for supplies the workers needed. The pages were glued together at the top and carbon paper had to be fitted between the pages. This was something the woman did not like to do and she handed the job to me. I had to type the numbers from my inventory paper onto this form, with a copy. I happened to make a mistake with the carbon paper, put it in the wrong way around between the second and third page and therefore the copy was on the backside of the previous page. The whole page was messed up and one could not mark what was actually to be listed on that page.

Oh my God! All hell broke loose. It was the only form this office would get and since it could not be used we could not order supplies until the next month. Short of being slapped on my head I was verbally abused and subsequently fired. My job experience was three weeks. My father was very upset and exclaimed, "I'll never lift a finger and help you find work again. This reflects on me and I don't like it. You were hired because of me and now I have egg on my face. I just hope there are no other consequences for me. I do want to keep my job."

Somehow I felt relieved but I was devastated for him. I knew it had not been the right job for me but I would not have given up. The next day Dad apologized and expressed the thought it might have been the best thing that could have happened.

"I didn't like the environment and when I heard some comments made about you being a delectable little thing I was sorry I even let you work there."

13: Uprising of the Sheep

Well, they were not really sheep. But they all felt like it.
They had no rights. They had no tools, no nails, no paint, no
screws, nothing with which to do their jobs. But they did have a
job. Even if it meant they would sit around, tell jokes, or play
cards. They had to be careful not to talk about "the good old
days", a time when you could go and buy what you needed.
There were always "ears" around so they had learned "not to talk
about it".

Nobody was able to tell after "it" happened or how "it" had
started. On the 17th of June 1953, just like sheep, they were
suddenly all heading for the big gate at the entrance to the wharf.
My father was one of the over one thousand workers. Quietly,
with no shouting or any other signs of aggression they walked
along the pot-holed street leading into the city. It wasn't long
before police cars arrived with loud speakers and demanded they
should turn around and go back to their jobs. They kept walking,
with hanging heads, slumped shoulders and empty hands. Many
had tears running down their faces.

Soon the Russian Army, the "Best Friends of the Labourers"
turned up with tanks and trucks and teargas. The "sheep" were
herded into a Sports Stadium where I as a 'Sports Instructor'
usually tested the athletic abilities of the ones willing to receive
the Sport Achievement Badge "Bereit zur Arbeit und zur
Verteidigung des Friedens." ('Ready to work and to defend the
peace') Incredibly, this uprising was happening in most of the
larger cities in East Germany all at the same time. Needless to
say, this quiet revolution was defeated by the powers that were.

A few days later I was taking a class of young teenagers to
the gym. As their physical education teacher I had been obliged

to teach them "marching". They could just not get it and always mixed up their 'rows' like sheep. On this day with a 'curfew' in place, I had been instructed not to 'march' them. They drove me crazy because now they marched in a perfect column. I was unable to break them up. I walked on the sidewalk and pretended I had nothing to do with them.

I won't forget the 17th of June 1953. It took another 36 years until the ruling political system in East Germany failed. The 17th of June is now a National Holiday in a united Germany.

14: Learning to Kayak

It was the best thing that ever happened to me! Afred, a young man in charge of the kayak racing team, came to my office to get the permission stamps for the team to go to a regatta taking place in a different city. As I asked him questions he invited me to come to a training session and see if I would like to join the club. I accepted right away and his girlfriend Christa showed me how to get in and out of a kayak. Balancing wasn't easy as I was trying to sit in the narrow nut shell. When I mastered it without tipping over I was in love, - in love with the novelty of it and in love with the water. Christa also let me try out the two-seater KII. I became obsessed with kayaking. I was determined to be in the top group and secretly promised myself to become better than all the other girls. You know what?

It was only a year later when I won the District Championships in the KI over 500 and over 3.000 meters. Mind you, after the 3.000 meter race I fell out of the kayak as soon as I crossed the finishing line. Christa, my trainer and also my KII partner was disappointed because up to now she had won all the races. But, when we won the 500 and the 3000 meters in the KII, she was happy again.

We became very close friends. Even now, more than sixty years later we are still friends. Since we live on different continents contact is mostly by telephone. She saved nearly forty-five years of letters I wrote to her from Canada after my emigration in 1963. She gave them to me last time I saw her. To read them again was quite a revelation for me. It took a long time to read my own story in forty-five years of letters I had written. I read about my struggle during the first years in Canada. I read about periods when I had tried to convince myself I had done the right thing to marry a penfriend with a little daughter and leave Germany. I realized it had been an uphill struggle because of my feelings of responsibility towards, in time, two young girls under my care. I also came across a time when I had thought of ending my life. I had confessed to Christa about coming home one evening close to 10.30 and my husband, sitting in the dark kitchen, had asked me: "Where were you?" I told him I had been at the lake. He said "If you can do this to me I understand but how can you do this to the children? Their first mother ran away and if you leave them too you ruin them for life."

The best years within my first thirty years have to do with the water, my boat and my desolation in leaving it behind when I had to escape from East to West Germany to protect myself and especially my father. As it happened, my racing abilities helped me to find a job in West Germany. I never reached the top group again. I had to work too many hours and did not have as much time for the necessary training.

You might find it interesting to learn that in East Germany every sport was 'political' and very highly promoted and financially supported by the government. It hardly cost anything for either memberships or competitions. In West Germany you were on your own unless you had sponsors. As I earned very little money I could not afford to participate anymore. When I was fifth at a competition I decided to call it quits. I wanted people to remember me and say "Oh, she was good" rather than "Yeah, she got too old and had to drop out".

Did you know they now have real racing kayaks for kiddies? And start training them very early? Just like Austrian kids start to ski as soon as they can walk, at the Baltic Sea the kids can start at two or three years old getting into a child sized kayak. Amazing! Train our future Olympians! Yes, the children are our future in more ways than one. Kayaking is healthy, you breathe fresh air,

44

develop muscles but mainly around the upper body. Therefore training includes running, all-body exercises and during the winters we did gymnastics and played competitive table tennis. A very important thing: Comradery. I give it ten points out of ten. It's wonderful. Every sport connects and it becomes a big part of your life. Look at the soccer, hockey or other teams!

The years of kayaking were the best years of my life.

15: What Happened to Them?

Yesterday they were sleeping in four tents next to us. Today there was no sign, and I mean absolutely no sign of them. Did we just dream they were here?

We were camping on the beautiful Isle of Hiddensee in the Baltic Sea. Located between the mainland and the larger Isle of Rügen it was one of our kayak clubs favourite weekend and even holiday spots. Hiddensee is a long narrow island and you can walk from the high cliffs with the lighthouse facing the Isle of Rügen all the way down to the other end where it tapers out into sand banks, always having water on both sides. Starting to paddle or, with a good breeze able to hoist our five square metre sail, it would only take us between three and four hours from the boat house in Stralsund to Hiddensee. We would aim for about the middle of the island, a place called Neuendorf with the fishing harbour, surrounded by the typical brilliant white romantic thatched island homes. These houses with small windows were hunkered down low to let the constant wind blow over and above them. We had to start walking on a shallow sand bank for the last one or two kilometers and pull our boats until we hit deeper water again.

We were four girls in two boats and had two tents. We found a nice camping place adjacent to the nudist beach. We couldn't believe it when we saw fully uniformed policemen checking the passports of the nude people. Where do you carry a passport if you have no clothing on? We snickered and were probably right to think they were only there out of curiosity. While we were spending the rest of the day suntanning and swimming several other tents had gone up in a row next to us with five single kayaks placed upside down between them. Five very fit looking men in their twenties were organizing their blankets and cook ware. When they noticed us next to them they called "Want to have dinner with us? Just soup, - but good company as a side dish and music for dessert. Bring your own bowls and spoons though."

They spent several days exploring the island and the few shops in Neuendorf and Kloster, a pretty village closer to the high cliffs of Hiddensee. They came back with Zeiss binoculars, a good camera, a small compass and stop watches. We were wondering how they could carry so much money to buy all this expensive stuff! It was a long time before credit cards were

invented. They would sit on the dunes every night for hours and watch the military search light reaching out with bright long rays over the Baltic Sea, starting at the lighthouse and coming back across the sandbanks.

We girls planned to attend a costume dance and were busy picking beach grass and making grass skirts. Intrigued, they inquired what we were up to.

"Can we join you?" We were delighted and glad not having to walk home in the dark on our own after the dance. We made more grass skirts and with lipstick painted Indian designs on all our faces and bodies. The men had found seagull feathers to complete our costumes. We enjoyed a kind of dress rehearsal on the beach. A few drinks the boys had provided loosened our inhibitions. With lots of noise we entered the dance hall and celebrated with our own tribal dance. We 'scalped' a few people, and at the end won first prize. It was a bottle of rum. The boys disappointed us by saying 'good night' when we suggested sitting on the dunes with them and let the bottle go around. "Tomorrow is another day" were their parting words.

Tomorrow came and their camping places were empty. Tents gone, boats gone, not even a garbage bag was left. It was as if they had never been there. We questioned other campers but nobody had seen or heard anything. Even the fishermen in the small harbour had not noticed them.

What happened to them? How could they just disappear? No 'good bye' after the fun we had last night? And the dinners we had shared? What about the rum we wanted to drink today?

Two months later I received a postcard from Sweden and another week later a letter. During all those nights when they were sitting on the dunes they had been measuring the time it took the search light to pass and come back to move over our area. Their kayaks had been prepared and they had taken off in a hurry. They knew how many seconds they had until the search light came and they did 'the roll'. They also knew how long they had to be under water before they could come back up and continue paddling. They had to do this manoeuver quite a few times. After several hours they were way out on the Baltic and continued paddling to Bornholm, Denmark. From there they went to Sweden, happy they had made it to "Freedom". They were sorry they could not tell us and hoped we had enjoyed drinking the rum thinking and talking about them. Certainly we had been doing that! People disappearing had become part of life in East Germany. I still wonder if they would have asked us to come along if we had been able to do 'the roll'. They had tried to teach us. Our boats were not suited to it anyway. Plus, there was probably the suspicion we might report their plans.

You never knew who to trust.

16: Escape from your Country?

Can you think of any good reason to escape from your own country? I am not talking about criminal acts causing you to escape or hide or trying to avoid punishment. No, I am talking about not being able to breathe anymore, not being able to talk openly, always being afraid to say the wrong thing, even within your own family.

About 60.000 people escaped almost monthly from East Germany to West Germany for many years. A number of them lost their lives when shot by other East Germans, maybe their brothers, cousins, or friends, - boys who had grown up since the war ended in 1945 and they became part of the East German Police Force. It was quite similar to the unemployed young men in the 1930's lining up to join the new Nazi army.

Let me tell you why I escaped from East Germany.

I was a Phys Ed teacher. I loved my job and the school principal repeatedly reminded me that I was obliged to join the SED, the communist party. "How can you be a teacher if you are not able to pass on the ideology of communism and foster loyalty in your students to our brothers in the Soviet Union?" Without being a member you had no chance for advancement and risked your job security. But, so far, I had avoided signing up and had ignored the pressure.

On October 4th 1955 I was told to face the music or else. After talking to my father he advised me to leave East Germany like so many thousands of others already had. I couldn't even say "Good bye" to my mother after the evening meal. Early the next morning I took the train to Berlin. Just outside Berlin proper, in Bernau, everybody had to leave the train, line up at a table to have their ID Cards checked by police and then continue on with

the S-Bahn (city train) to the inner city. The city train still
stopped at some West Berlin stations. Waiting for my papers to
be checked, the city train pulled in. When it started moving again
I lost my nerve and without thinking started running towards it.
The police had strict shooting orders for people trying to escape.
Two shots were fired. They missed, either by accident or by
design. I will never know. If witnesses claimed they missed on
purpose the shooter would be severely punished, put in jail or
even shot. Two Berliner men held the automatically closing train
doors open and pulled me into the last wagon. We expected the
train to be stopped. It wasn't.

Those two Berliners told me to get out at the next station
which happened to be in the "West Sector". I had to wait for
another train, one not going through the "East Sector", to
Marienfelde. This was the place where one had to register the
escape to West Berlin. I was thunderstruck by the long line-up of
people. Hundreds of them! Everybody who had escaped this day
was in line, yet it was only early in the afternoon. Most had no
luggage at all or, like me, only a small bag. Some didn't even
have jackets or coats. I moved forward with a young dental
assistant, a nice girl who hoped to be sent to the Black Forest.
She had relatives there. I had no idea where I would end up.

We stuck together and were given a bunk bed in a room with
only five other bunk beds in one of the many barracks for
escapees. I took the upper bed and kept my coat on top of my
blanket and my shoes close to the wall. We had been warned to
look after our few belongings because things "disappeared".
Most other rooms had fifteen or more bunk beds. We felt very
lucky. But don't even ask about bathrooms or showers. It was all
well organized, but very simple. There was an air of relief, but
not much talking. After our experiences in East Germany nobody
trusted anybody. We were afraid to say anything. What if the

Russians were coming? They were only a few kilometers away. Maybe there was an informer amongst us?

Most girls in our room were "processed" within a few days. Everyday new ones were occupying the beds. I was the only one kept there for three weeks. We had been told on Oct. 5th more than 16.000 people had escaped, not all through Berlin. I was repeatedly interviewed by the Americans, the English and French officers but in the end I could not tell them more than I already had. Actually, through their questions, I learned about military installations I had not even imagined on the Island of Rügen, my home for the past ten years. Finally they decided to fly me out to Hanover. My final destination was supposed to be Dortmund. My first flight was not exactly a flight into the sunset but what all of us thought of as FREEDOM. New challenges were awaiting me in the "golden West" as we "Ossies" ("Easties") called it. It was tough to learn our education in the east counted for nothing. We were considered second class citizens. At least it was what we were made to feel.

You want to know what happened on October 4th that drove me to leave my family, my hometown, the job I enjoyed, my beloved boat and my kayaking friends? The principal of our school promised to 'protect' me and my family if I would agree to sleep with him. He hinted he was aware of my father's Siberian experiences and that he was the real reason for me not joining the party. He could report us.

"You have no choice" he had yelled after me when I grabbed my bike and raced off.

17: J.F.Kennedy Assassination

November 22nd 1963 12.30 PM: It is almost impossible to believe over fifty years have gone by since the world was rocked by the assassination of the 35th President of the United States. J.F.Kennedy was smiling at the people lined up along the road. He was riding in an open car with his beautiful wife Jackie beside him passing through the Dealey Plaza in Dallas and hundreds of onlookers saw him collapse suddenly. A couple of shots were fired. Hundreds of conspiracy theories and many inquiries into his death were never resolved; the why and by whom. Was it the lone shooter Harvey Lee Oswald who was originally arrested for shooting the officer J.D. Tippit and then was, himself, shot within two days, or was it an international plot, or a group of people? There are no final answers to the many questions to this very day.

Four other Presidents have been shot before J.F. Kennedy:

Abraham Lincoln was assassinated in 1865, James Garfield in 1881, William McKinley in 1901 and Warren G. Harding in 1923.

Did you know shooting an American President was not a Federal Offence until 1965?

Do you remember where you were when J.F.K. was shot? Do you remember what and how you felt when you heard the news? I do: I was having breakfast in a small restaurant in Saarbruecken/Germany and the next bite literally got stuck in my throat. I never finished my meal. Every guest put down their eating utensils. A surreal silence enveloped everybody with only the news reporter's announcements on the radio searing through our brains. We could not comprehend nor accept what was being said. What? Why!? For heaven's sake, why? Many people in the restaurant started crying. It was as if everybody's best friend had suddenly been killed. Nobody left, everybody was sitting as if nailed to their chairs for hours.

I remember JFK's famous exclamation during a speech in Berlin: "Ich bin ein Berliner!" It wasn't just the Berliners who loved him for it. - The Berliners suffered under tight restrictions living in a divided city, the Berliners who remembered the blockade of their city by the Eastern block and who remembered the western military aircraft landing every few minutes at the inner city "Tempelhof "Airport to bring not only food but fuel and everything else the city needed to function for almost a whole year. The Americans kept the western "sectors" of Berlin alive. Otherwise the Berliners would have had no choice but to succumb to the Communist pressure and become part of the Eastern Block. After all, Berlin was an "Island" within East Germany.

J.F.Kennedy stood for the dream that was 'America' – and the very word and everything associated with it spelled "Freedom".

And now the President of America had been shot. This man, liked the world over, was shot. The western world had lost a great leader, loved and admired and now mourned by millions. Who could forget the photograph of the small little son who stood at attention and paid his respect to his dad when the coffin was carried by? It still drives tears to my eyes. Poor little guy.

There are certain happenings in our life which are indelible, impossible to forget. For me, others would be the death of Princess Diane and the airplanes flying into the twin towers in New York. On both occasions I sat glued to my favorite chair for hours on end, watching the happenings over and over and over...

Each time was like a bad dream. Only I couldn't wake up.

18: She got Away – but only 'just'

Edith is my youngest sister. She recently celebrated her 70th birthday. I telephoned her on this occasion and mentioned the fact my memoir had just been published. "Did you include the story of my drowning?"

"Your drowning? When did that happen? This is the first I ever heard of it. How did you survive?"

Our sister Christel had escaped from East Germany in 1956, a year after I did. As was required by the West German authorities she surrendered her East German passport pending issuance of a West German one. During this interval she received first a telegram, then a letter from home stating "Edith has drowned, come home immediately". Without having travel documents she was in no position to "go home" but was, quite naturally, most upset to learn of our youngest sister's unexpected demise.

Months later our father got a visa and went to visit Christel in Hamburg. If he failed to return it was one less pension to be paid. Christel met him at the train station with a black band around her coat sleeve. Father asked why on earth she wore that, whereupon she burst into tears and said it was because of Edith's death. Father was astounded to learn of his youngest daughter's drowning. He had left her at the train station at home earlier that morning. Christel explained about the telegram and showed him the letter. He recognized the writing as that of a neighbour living in the attic suite above his home. It became evident this neighbour was a 'Stasi' agent, an informer.

The telegram and the letter had been a ruse to get Christel to return home where she would have faced years of imprisonment for having defected to the west. What a lucky escape she had.

Why had I never heard about this before? Is this another instance of "We don't talk about that"?

19: Olympic Games

Olympic Games are always exciting. Let's remember several 'outstanding' Olympics: The Summer Games in Berlin 1936 and the Winter Games in Sochi 2014 and several in-between leaving a mark.

While watching the Winter Olympics in Sochi I couldn't help but think of the 1936 Olympics in Berlin. I was just a small kid but people talked about it for years because something too unusual had happened. One was the new 'Glider competition' (never repeated at other games) and the other, huge one making a furore was the first black-skinned man running like nobody ever did before.

I like to compare some historic political facts: In 1936 Hitler wanted to show the world a recovering Germany after WWI. In 2014 Putin put on an incredible show with state-of-the-art venues to show the world the "New Russia". For both leaders their Olympics are "Memorials" and are forever connected to their names.

Adolf Hitler, watching the games surrounded by his officers and body guards, shook every Gold Medal Winner's hand as they walked up to him. An unexpected medalist, a black man, Jesse Owens from the US, won the first of four gold medals in the 100 meter dash. The world press reported Hitler stormed out of the stadium, angry how a 'sub-human' could beat his Aryan superb athletes. It was the accepted version of what happened that day.

Jesse Owens was a huge surprise at the Berlin Olympic Games in 1936. One surprise was his skin color and the other was his running ability to win four gold medals.

It wasn't until the sixties when the journalist Siegfried Mischner at 83 years old wrote a book about the 1936 Olympics.

He reported Jesse Owens had shown him a photo he carried in his wallet with Hitler shaking his hand. Jesse had declared:

"It was my proudest moment. I was treated better in Germany than I was in the US where we blacks faced segregation."

Apparently the photo was not taken in front of the world press but behind the honour stand. Jesse Owens died in 1980 but always claimed he had not been snubbed by Hitler, but rather the world press had been reluctant to make the monster Adolf Hitler look good. Mr. Mischner wanted to set the record straight before he died and stated other journalists had seen the photo as well. Most people still believe the original version of what happened.

Let's also take a look at some of the other memorable summer games. The next games after 1936 were supposed to be in Tokyo in 1940. In 1938 Japan tried to get permission for a postponement but the games had to be cancelled. The country was supposed to build the venues out of wood since the metal was needed for war preparations. Tokyo promised to hold the games as soon as peace was restored but it did not happen until 1964.

Traditionally the games are held every four years. It was twelve years after the Berlin Olympics when London wanted to demonstrate to the world "the worst is over". They applied for, and were awarded, the first Olympic Summer Games after the war in 1948. Food rationing was still in effect. Athletes received 5.500 calories compared to 2.600 for ordinary people. The athletes were asked to buy or make their own uniforms. No new venues or special athlete's villages were built. London based athletes commuted from their homes. International female athletes were housed in colleges and males in military camps.

Germany and Japan, seen as the WWII aggressors, were not invited while Russia was but did not send any competitors. Fifty-

nine nations with a total of 4.104 athletes (90% males) competed
and the total cost was £730.000. The games became known as the
"Austerity Games." Compare the numbers to the London Games
in 2012: 10.000 athletes participated from 204 nations. Total cost
was £8.92 billion. The 2012 London Olympic Games are thought
of as "the best Olympics ever".

Helsinki Finland had its chance in 1952. Melbourne
Australia in 1956, Rome 1960 and the not so ordinary happening
here was the surprise that the two Germanys agreed to the IOC
request to send only one team. East and West Germany
participated with a "United Team of Germany." The East was
proud their athletes won more medals than the West. True, and in
my opinion it is due to the fact that East Germany promoted and
paid for sports involvement and special training for Olympians.
In West Germany sport was much more expensive and poor
athletes could not even afford to join clubs or get the needed
funds for extensive training. Tokyo finally organized the games
in 1964 and Mexico City in 1968.

The next games, the Olympic Games in Munich in 1972
went down in history for the horrific "Munich massacre." Eleven
Israeli athletes and a German Police Officer were killed by
Palestinian terrorists. Ironically, unsuspecting Canadian athletes
coming home late climbed over the six foot fence of the Olympic
Village. They noticed and helped eight track-suit clad men with
their bags to get over the fence. These were the terrorists who
targeted the Israeli team. They got into their apartments. They
took hostages while two fought them and were shot dead right
away. To the offers of any amount of money and free passage
home during negotiations they answered:

"Money and our life mean nothing to us."

They demanded 234 Palestinians and non-Arabs to be set
free by Israel plus two German terrorists, infamous Andreas

Baader and Ulrike Meinhoff, who had formed the "Red Army Faction". They were held in Germany. Both countries denied the request. Further negotiations lead to providing helicopters and a Lufthansa plane for the terrorists at the Munich Airport for a safe passage to Cairo. Germany, according to its post-war constitution, had been unable to include the army in the security measures and was not prepared for a terrorist attack. The Munich Police were overwhelmed; a plan involving sharp shooters went awry, the helicopter carrying the hostages was blown up by the terrorists, five of whom were killed, the other three captured and released immediately after a Pan Am plane kidnapping. I found the whole very detailed story online under "Munich Massacre 1972." I could hardly stomach it. Talk about the German slogan for the games:

"Carefree Games."

Wait, there is more! What intrigued me and was enjoyed by the whole wide world was the fact that one of the pretty hostesses, Silvia Sommerlath met the Crown Prince Carl Gustaf of Sweden during the games. They were spotted together repeatedly and when the pesky journalists caught up with the prince and asked about his relationship with a commoner he answered "it was love at first sight." They were married in 1976. Silvia captured the hearts of the Swedes. They had three children during the following years: Two little princesses and a prince.

As soon as it had been possible the games in 1972 continued as 'The show must go on' - with a fairy tale ending to the most gruesome Olympics for one happy couple who

"Lived happily ever after."

20: The 'Beheaded' Rose

Hannes. I met Hannes two months too late. Had we met two months earlier something might have become of it. Maybe. Maybe not. He had such an infectious laugh, such as I had never heard from a man and never did again. I knew he would never do or try something I would not want. He was 'comfortable' like an old pair of shoes, more like a brother and I felt at ease when I was with him. I still kept him at arm's length. Why? There were several reasons:

One, I was afraid I could fall in love with him.

Two, he was in the middle of a divorce even it was a friendly one.

Three, he was from the Rhineland and the Rhinelanders had a reputation for being 'light weights', people who didn't take life too seriously.

Fourth, he was Catholic and I was Lutheran, a match my parents would not approve of, even if neither of us were religious church goers.

Fifth, I was in love with a little girl in Canada who needed a new mommy. Her father and I had been penfriends for two months and he wanted to marry me.

But the main reason was I was afraid, simply afraid that a man who was obsessed with me, who had stalked me for years would be true to his promise to ruin any relationship I would ever have with another man. "If I can't have you, nobody else will." I had told Hannes all about it. Hannes listened, talked to me and made me see all sides. He pointed out the pros but mainly the cons about going to Canada. He sounded exactly like my father who thought I had gone totally bananas. "Canada! Marry a man you don't know, divorced and with a daughter? Nuts!" The problem was my compassion for the little girl when I saw the photos of her with the sad eyes. I just couldn't get her out of my mind. Once I had met her grandparents in Wiesbaden I was lost. They didn't even give me a chance to back out. They were very persuasive. I didn't realize I was being manipulated. The word did not exist in my vocabulary or my thinking.

Hannes became my best friend. He helped me plan my emigration. We went to the zoo in Hamburg, to a fabulous Indian Restaurant and sampled the "Indian Rice Table" with twenty-three little bowls containing different delectable types of food. We visited the "Pferdestall" a famous kind of pub/bar in an original horse barn. We attended "A Midsummer Night's Dream" on the stage under the stars in the Herrenhäuser Gardens in Hanover. When I started to get very involved with the emigration requirements, health check- ups, the sale of my belongings and my Canadian penfriend and his parents, sadly my friendship with Hannes somehow tapered out. It was the end of a time with lots of laughter for me but I didn't realize it until much, much later.

When I was living in Winnipeg in Canada I got terribly homesick. I wrote to Hannes telling him about my life. He had married a lady he had seen in the theatre. He wrote "I had noticed her legs and they reminded me of you." He had approached her during intermission, they had a glass of champagne and the rest is history. Hannes and I remained in occasional letter contact.

A few years later I visited Germany. I had arranged a meeting with the last company I worked for since I wanted to import their skin care line to Canada. I had been instrumental in developing a number of the products. Before flying home I planned to visit my sister in Hamburg and since Hannes lived there he picked me up at the train station. He handed me a beautiful long stemmed dark red 'Baccara Rose'. We walked across the busy plaza in front of the station to his parked car.

After he put my suitcase in the trunk he opened the door for me. We both were a bit shy, not yet at ease as we had been during the two months in the past when we had laughed a lot. I held the rose and my purse with one hand, trying to arrange my fancy coat which had a split in the back so the two sides could be lifted and I would not sit on it. I changed the flower from my left to my right hand and arranged the coat around me with the other. Finally I was seated with both coat tails on my lap. Hannes asked "is everything in now?" We looked at each other when I replied, "Yes, everything is in". He closed the door and walked around the car to his side. As he was inserting the car key I noticed I had only the stem of the rose in my hand. I felt the shock right down into my tummy:

"Hannes, look" I whispered with a tiny voice. Hannes grabbed his steering wheel, put his head on his arms and slowly, quietly said "Just like us. It's our story. A beheaded love story, a beheaded rose... I should have seen the rose wasn't in when I closed the door. Should we stop by a flower shop and I'll buy you a new one?"

We decided against it. After a while driving along Hannes started to laugh. His Rhineland humour had taken over and he thought the whole episode was really very funny. I was sorry to have lost the beautiful flower head but I tried to see the humour in it as well.

Actually, because of the accident, - I never forgot the rose. Or Hannes.

21: A Heart Wrenching, Sad Love Story

Maybe it's not my place to tell it. But who else can tell it? The two people involved cannot tell it and the others old enough to know the story have died and the younger ones don't really remember the way it was. The story is about my third sister, Ingrid, who had been such an easy going baby and child of whom people said: "Yes, later children are much easier." I was six years old when Ingrid was born and had decided right then and there I would only have "later children". Our mother always admonished the rest of us: "Look at Ingrid! She is never ever sick! And the rest of you come up with something every time I turn around."

We were four girls, each one destroying our father's hope for a boy. It wasn't meant to be. After the war he confessed "I am so glad for my girls. At least they won't be cannon fodder in the next war." I, the oldest and the third, Ingrid, had Mother's hazel greenish eyes and the second and the fourth, Christel and Edith, were born with our father's deep blue eyes. There also was a special connection within the two pairs. That's why I know Ingrid's story. We were very much alike in our looks, our likes, our thinking and our love of sports and books.

It was at my nineteenth birthday party, my very first party ever. There were twenty of my canoe club friends plus our family of six. We were having fun, cooking pancakes on my new camping stove, flipping them over in the air and not always catching them, and a lot of laughter caused by some homemade wine. Late in the evening I started to "read palms", telling fortunes and Ingrid was the last one who asked: "Can you read mine too?" Naturally I took a look and without thinking told her "For a start, you won't have a long life. Your lifeline is very short…" She was only thirteen at the time. I shut up, shocked by my insensitivity. I could not shake a weird sense of premonition.

"Will I still marry before I die?" I knew what I saw but told her little white lies. At least I saw it that way. After all, this was just fun. I really didn't know much about the "science" of telling fortunes. Not much later the party broke up.

Ingrid was fifteen when my parents told me she was seeing Benno, a boy of whom they did not approve. Benno was a year or two older than Ingrid but he was into drinking and always into fist fights with other boys. His parents could not handle him but he loved his grandma who lived next door to us. He often came to stay with her. I asked Ingrid "Why Benno? There are so many other nice boys around" - but she said "He needs me. With me he is nice. He talks and he doesn't drink. Nobody else understands him. I see no reason why I should not see him. We are good friends."

Ingrid was an athlete and her fortè was swimming and diving. She had joined a swimming club and became a fantastic breast stroke swimmer. She also was a member of the diving team. Plus, she was in charge of the warm-up exercises for the younger members.

In early July the following summer she was chosen for a children's camp as a "sport teacher's assistant." After about a week she was sent home because of an unexplained terrible pain in her right shoulder. She could not even lift her arm to comb her hair. She was told by the family doctor not to train, not to swim, rest the arm and in general not to overdue anything. The pain did not go away. It got worse and at the end of August Dad took her to a private doctor. After a thorough examination his diagnosis was a shock: Suspected Youth Sarcoma. He told my father to immediately take her to the Charitè in Berlin, a famous special hospital. Within three days her right arm was amputated, right out

68

of the shoulder joint. More tests revealed the cancer had already gone into the shoulder blade and collarbone. She refused to have those bones removed as well.

Her statement was "I am already crippled enough; no boy will ever love me and I know I have to die anyway." Six weeks later she returned home. Aunt Irene, a former army nurse came daily to renew the bandages and make sure she had enough painkiller pills. Ingrid refused morphine.

"I want to die with my mind intact. I don't want to be a vegetable."

Ingrid with friends in Berlin without her right arm.

Benno had given up drinking and my parents allowed him to make regular visits. By early December Ingrid's cancer had grown out of the shoulder cavity as if a new arm was growing, all the way up to the elbow. The pain grew worse and she was taken into the local hospital. When Christmas was just a week away my parents asked her if she had a special wish. I lived in West Germany and kept sending items they could not get in East Germany: Chocolate, oranges, lemons; my parents would send a telegram with what Ingrid would like to have. I cried a lot during those weeks and once almost caused an accident with a bus and a car because I biked right into them. I couldn't see for my tears...

Ingrid had only one Christmas wish: To come home, lie in her own bed to die. The doctors warned my parents, advised against it because it would be the hardest thing they would ever do in their lives; they might not be able to stand it. They were adamant and insisted on granting Ingrid's wish. They did. They knew it would be her last wish.

Benno gave her a beautifully wrapped present, a long fancy night gown. It made her happy and sad at the same time. He told her he would wait for her and marry her when she got well, it didn't matter that she only had one arm, he still had two and they would manage. My parents were upset about the fancy night gown, thought it inappropriate but there was nothing they could do about it. Ingrid had several good days during which she read a book I had sent her. I don't remember the title. I had read it as well; it was something about five lives we each have of which the last one was about the afterlife. I had been impressed by its sensual spirituality. Mother wrote in a letter: "Ingrid told me to let you know it gave her hope and she is not afraid of dying anymore."

During January her pain was so bad Aunt Irene, when injecting her pain medication mixed in a little morphine without telling Ingrid. It helped to ease her plight a bit without clouding her mind; yet sadly, the cancer had taken over her whole body.

On February 5th her fight with this horrible cancer, the same as one of the Kennedy boys had, was over. She died and was buried dressed in the night gown Benno had given her. He was totally devastated, started drinking heavily and three weeks after her funeral he hanged himself.

70

August 4th is her birthday. She loved gladiolas. I always buy a bunch and think of her. There is no grave I can take them to – they are on my coffee table. It is 2015 and she would be seventy-five years old this year but I cannot imagine her as an old woman.

She is forever the young seventeen year old girl I loved so much.

22: Cuba, Cora and Secrets Revealed

It was just a year after I had moved myself and the wholesale part of my business from Winnipeg in the Canadian Prairies to beautiful British Columbia and, to top it off, to the coveted life in the city of West Vancouver. It was 1985 and during those years not everybody had a copier, a fax machine and certainly not a computer. I was lucky because around the corner from my office an elegant, beautiful white haired lady had a small business providing all those services to other small businesses like mine. We started visiting over a cup of coffee when I came to her and waited for my papers. One day I told her I was flying to Cuba for a holiday.

"Cuba? Really? That's interesting. When are you going?" When I answered "tomorrow" she sat back in her chair and asked "Do you go by yourself or share a room with someone? Or don't you do that kind of thing? In case you do, would you mind if I tag along? If I can still get a ticket?"

An hour later she phoned me:

"It's settled. I got the last seat on the plane".

And that is how I got to know one of the most interesting and unforgettable women in my life. Cuba had opened up for Canadian visitors in 1966 and this was my second visit. I knew

the Cuban maids doing our room would be delighted if we brought pencils and pantyhose because these were rare. We were placed in the (former) Beach House of the Kennedy family. We shared a very large room. My only complaint about Cora was that she read all night. I like it to be dark. We talked a lot. She told me about her incredible life in South Africa. She had immigrated to Canada because of an affair with a married man. She desperately needed to get away from him since she saw no joint future and just heartache if she stayed. As you can imagine, we got to know each other quite well.

Back in Vancouver I developed terrible back pain. Cora referred me to her massage therapist whom she had seen for years. "He has the magic touch", she told me, and she was right. I became a regular in his practice. He had two stepdaughters and his tales often reminded me of my similar former life.

West Vancouver had a famous vegetarian health food store with a restaurant. "Capers" served the most delicious food and at lunch the crowds where always lining up. Often I met there with other business ladies, sharing jokes and laughing our heads off. On one of those occasions I saw Cora standing there, looking around as if searching for someone. I jumped up, greeted her and she said "I am supposed to meet my son here…" I was dumb founded because she had never mentioned she had a son. At that moment my massage therapist came in, saw us, greeted us and then also looked around and said "You two won't believe it, but I am to meet my birthmother here. I was adopted and I have been searching for her."

Cora paled, stared at him and said "YOU? I came here to meet my son…"

Phil, the massage therapist who had massaged her for years, also cried out "YOU? YOU are my birth mother?"

Cora had told me so much of her life when we shared a room in Cuba but this was a story she had never, ever talked about. She had sadly mentioned she had absolutely no family. Now, when we met the next time, she smiled her beautiful smile, lighting up her whole face:

"Giselle, first I had nobody for more than fifty years and now I have a son, a daughter in law and grandchildren. Can you believe it?" She organized a big celebration on her large deck and all her small business customers were invited. Talking among us we were all incredulous and just kept looking at her:

Our beaming and gracious hostess, Cora.

23: Coffee? Black, White, Cookie?

I remember Fred C. He had quite a story to tell. He was born in England around 1896 or 1897 to a very frail mother. She deteriorated over the next few years and couldn't look after him. At only five years old he had seen the inside of several foster homes. He ran away when he was seven but got caught, and when he was just nine he ran away again. This time he was successful and sneaked onto a freighter ship in London UK where he hid in a lifeboat. He was discovered when far out at sea and was put to work shovelling coal to earn his keep.

"It didn't matter that I was just a kid, I had to work. I knew lots of kids at my age worked in mines in England."

He was ninety-four years old when we met. It was in a bank in West Vancouver. I was sharing a cup of coffee and a cookie with a friend visiting from Germany when he turned away from the banking counter, stopped, looked at us and commented "Hmm, two beautiful ladies drinking coffee?" I smiled at him. He was a slightly stooped old man with a cane, a jocular face with a goatee and a handle bar moustache.

"You want a coffee too? Come, sit down with us, I will fix it for you! Black or white, sugar? Cookie?" His suit was slightly soiled, his pants baggy but he still had something imposing about him. 'Commodore' flitted through my mind.

"Hmm" he said, stroking his goatee, "I would have to ask my mother. It's one thing to have coffee and cookies but to sit down with two beautiful ladies? She might take my skate board away!"

We couldn't help it. We broke out in joyful laughter. Imagining this old man on a skate board was just too funny. He sat down with us and for three hours we told jokes. He finished one, I would tell another and I bet the bankers had never had such a happy afternoon. I cautioned him that we were disturbing the tellers, but they yelled "No, we love it" and Fred warned "Oh, if they make me leave I'll take all my money with me."

It was the beginning of a great friendship. I invited him to every party in my home and he took me out for a meal in a restaurant once a month. He always startled the waiters with something. Once, when asked if he would like dessert he pointed at me and whispered "I'll have to ask my mother..." and the waiter stared at me in shock. There were forty years between us. I took him out for his 99th birthday and had asked the restaurant staff to sing "Happy Birthday" for him. I had told them he was ninety-nine. Fred had brought a birthday card he had received from my German friend who was a graphic designer, cleverly done with the 99 in such a way the card could be turned around so that it said 66. He had placed it on our table showing the '66'. I was called to the counter and the headwaiter admonished me for "exaggerating". Well, old Fred surely did not look 66 by any means, but the young waiters had no age concept. After some discussion they did sing after all and actually the whole restaurant sang along.

When Fred turned 100 years old, we had dinner in the fine 'Salmon House' in West Vancouver. When we were ready to leave the waiter mentioned he would bring the check. Fred, with a sneaky face, asked "Can't I rather have the money?"

Over the years I had often urged him to tell me more of his life story. I offered to write his memoir since he did not want to do it.

"Oh Giselle", he said, looking at me, "I don't like to talk about it." But each time we met he inadvertently told me something and it added up to quite a lot.

78

Fred was very gratuitous towards the Salvation Army. They had been the ones who had taken him under their wing when the freighter had docked in Halifax.

"I was a lost and lonely nine-year-old kid standing on the shores of Halifax in Canada."

His eyes had the sentimental expression of people looking back into their past. The Salvation Army placed him with a farmer's family outside of the city where he had to earn his bread and butter before and after school. When Fred was fifteen the farmer got involved in selling Life Insurance Policies. He 'sold' one to Fred and deducted the premium from the little allowance he received for incidentals. At sixteen he ran away again and this time was lucky to be taken in by a Jewish stock broker. While he was urged to finish school he helped with filing and other office work. Once he had to sign one not quite legal deal since his boss did not want to use his own name. It turned out alright and for the first time he was paid more than just a little money. When he told me this story he was remembering how scared he had been.

"I owe him a lot. Everything I know about investing I learned from that man."

Fred lived an incredible life in Canada. He worked on Parliament Hill for more than twenty years, "Behind the scenes". With more power than the Prime Minister," he stated. He fought with Canada during WWI and retired with the title Commodore.

"In Flanders fields the poppies blow
between the crosses, row on row
That mark our place;
and in the sky the larks, still bravely singing,
fly - scarce heard amid the guns below.
We are the Dead.
Short days ago we lived, felt dawn, saw sunset glow,

Loved and were loved, and now we lie
In Flanders fields.
Take up our quarrel with the foe.
To you from failing hands we throw the torch;
be yours to hold it high.
If ye break faith with us who die
we shall not sleep, though poppies grow
In Flanders fields."

I heard this touching poem for the first time from Fred and it brought tears to my eyes. He 'acted' it. He knew it by heart.

The Canadian Government invited him to fly to Europe with several other over hundred year old veterans to visit Flanders Field on 55th anniversary of D-Day. He declined, claiming he did not have a passport. Three days later a government official and a photographer knocked on his door at the care home and 24 hours later he had a passport. A young cadet was assigned to look after him and they were flown to Ottawa for a few days with quite a program each day. In Flanders Fields he was the proud Canadian flag carrier shown on the front page of a Belgian Newspaper. He proudly showed it to me.

"I was not the oldest one", he said, "The oldest man in our group was one-hundred-and-fifteen years old. He was in a wheel chair. He couldn't carry the flag."

They were a group of about a dozen veterans, flown out of Ottawa in an aircraft outfitted with beds. Each one had his own cadet to look after their every need. A doctor and several nurses were also on board. Fred smiled his mischievous smile, told me how he had outrageously flirted with one of the nurses and that he had proposed to her, a forty-two year old woman with a terrific sense of humour. When I saw Fred after his return he joked: "Sorry, my dear, I cannot shake your hand. I haven't washed mine for two weeks. Three queens have shaken my hand. I kissed the hand of one, and I will not wash any of the memories off. Not even for you."

That was Fred C., a serious man but always joking. Memories of him came back recently after looking at old war time photographs and listening to the reports of D-Day 2014 with old and new images taken by journalists.

There was more to Fred. During his working years in Ottawa he had also been the President of the "Ottawa best dressed Men's Club." I was incredulous but he, with a twinkle in his old eyes, insisted such a club had once existed.

"I was also a Sunday School Teacher, you know? Can you tell me how a camel gets through the eye of a needle?"

No, it's just a bible fable.

"No dear, it is true. Cities during ancient times had a wall around them and the big gates were closed at night. A small little door was next to it. It was called the 'eye of the needle' and if a citizen came home late he had to make himself known to the gate keeper who would open the 'eye of the needle' and let him and his crouching camel in."

Fred's bible had lots and lots of notes placed throughout. I told him I would love for him to leave me his bible when he departs on his last trip. He lived for a number of years in a care home. He had started a choir and especially all the ladies loved him dearly. He died just a week short of his 102nd Birthday. It happened at lunch when he was seated at a table with three other men. He was in the middle of telling a joke. Before he came to the punch line he started to giggle, followed by laughing, laughter turned into coughing and – he fell from the chair and could not be revived. It was a perfect ending of Fred's life. Nobody got to know the punchline of his last joke. And no, I did not receive the bible.

I so wish I could share my book "We Don't Talk About That" with him.

24: "Would you like to marry me?"

We met Ed and Lucy on a Panama Cruise. The four of us shared a dining table with another couple. I cannot remember their names or faces. They never stayed after dinner. In their presence we did not talk much. Ed and Lucy were elderly darlings. It was touching to see how tenderly Ed helped Lucy. He pulled out her chair, put a scarf around her shoulders, held her elbow when walking in and out of the dining room and always had his warm, shining eyes on her.

A historian was talking about the building of the Panama Canal over a loudspeaker while we sailed through it. Everybody crowded around the railing at the bow. We were jostling to take photographs. I remember how badly I needed to go to the restroom but didn't dare to leave and lose my spot. We stood out there for hours while the voice over the speaker was droning on. Ed had found a place in a corner with an exhaust funnel big enough for Lucy to sit on top. He had lifted her up there like a child and kept her safe, his arms around her. Lucy was glowing, and she was smiling at everyone. Whenever we met them on land they always held hands. He would buy her a single rose which she would pin on her dress or jacket when coming to dinner. During my teenage years I had thought this kind of tenderness a bit silly. In later years I was touched almost to tears when I saw older people holding hands. Did I feel jealous because I never had this kind of attention? No, I felt sad and I wished... I asked a trusted male friend why this never happened to me. He told me "You seem too confident. You don't need a man to take care of you. Men instinctively know that. No man would dare to just do it. It would have to come from you."

Hmmm... Once, at a convention in New Orleans coming from breakfast, a gentleman in our group grabbed my hand when we crossed the street. I pulled it free as soon as we were on the other side. He looked at me and said "You don't like holding hands, do you?"

Back to Ed and Lucy: After dinner was ordered they would hold hands either under or even on top of the table. I noticed their legs under the table were always touching. When feeling more comfortable with them I mentioned my admiration for the display of their apparent love. Smiling, they looked at each other, Lucy nodded and Ed told us their story.

They were both widowed. Together they had been married a total of a hundred-and-eight years, albeit to different partners. She came from a large family and still had six living siblings, the oldest 82, the youngest 71. She was 78 and her next younger brother was 77 years old and not well. Ed was 79 and alone since he had lost his wife. They lived in the same city in Florida but had never met. A good friend of Ed's felt sorry for him. He invited Ed to come to his church in another part of the city to join a group of people who met once a month for coffee. Ed happened to be placed next to Lucy. He mentioned "I was very shy and quiet. Lucy was an extrovert. She helped me to feel relaxed. We had a lovely time. When the social broke up I was afraid I would never see her again and dared to ask her:

84

"Would you like to meet me for coffee tomorrow?"

She had looked at him for a few long seconds and he started to lose heart. But finally she said:

"Yes I would."

Again they had a good time. He told her he was able to cook a real good spaghetti dinner. When she laughed and looked at him expectantly he asked:

"Would you like to come to dinner at my house on Saturday?"

Again she let him wait for a few seconds and then just told him:

"Yes, I would."

The dinner, three days later, was a success. He showed her the house, photographs of his late wife, they laughed a lot and before she left he asked her:

"Would you….would you like to marry me?"

She looked at him for a long time. He was afraid he had been too hasty. But then, a big smile spreading across her face, she said:

"Yes, I would".

The old gentleman looked lovingly at Lucy, held her hand across the table and Lucy continued the story. "We were married three weeks later, are married for a week now and are on our honeymoon."

Their story brought tears to my eyes.

It was in Curacao, on the coast of South America. We arrived back at the ship after a tour but had to wait for a bellhop with luggage, followed by Ed and Lucy, coming down the gangway. Lucy was crying. I was asking why they were leaving and was sad to hear why their honeymoon had been cut short. Her younger brother had died and they needed to go home for his funeral. I hugged both of them, said God Speed and Ed whispered to me:

"Don't be sad for us, I'll take her on another honeymoon. Soon."

Now, in my "golden years" myself, I understand their kind of love. Cupid's arrow hits independent of age. Isn't it comforting to know? We have to make each day count. None of us knows how much time we have left.

"Yesterday is gone, tomorrow not here yet. All we have is today."

25: A Letter to Cindy

My dear little Cindy: For a long time you have been on my mind. I want to write about my thoughts and maybe feel a little closer to you. I won't ask you the typical question 'how are you' because I know you cannot answer it. But sharing my memories is another matter. Memories are the only way to connect and not let somebody you loved so much, die. I will not go into beliefs about an 'after-life' and the hope to see everybody again: My granny, my parents, my sister Ingrid who had to die so young and several of my dearest friends. But I do have to admit I have had moments when an almost wild joy flooded my veins thinking it might just be possible.

Cindy, I will never forget how much you loved me. You were always there for me. I still wonder how you knew when I needed you most – but you always did. My tears were flowing copiously when I read the book about the two brothers sailing, their boat capsizing and one held onto the hand of the other until finally the hand slipped away and only the younger brother survived, sitting on top of the boat. The elder boy was the darling of his mother, she blamed the young lad and never forgave him, the marriage broke up, the boy needed counselling, - it was a heartbreaking story.

Cindy, my dear little Cindy, you sat close to my legs, kept cuddling closer and then you put your little head on my knees and when I did not stop crying you pushed it up between me and my book, looked at me and stopped me from reading. Another day, I came home from work, totally exhausted, made it up the stairs and lay down on the blue Tunisian carpet in the fetal position to ease my back. You lay down next to me and looked right into my eyes. When I turned around to ease my other side, you walked around me and again, lay down and looked at me. We did not need words.

Or all those mornings, when I would sit at my office desk, deal with letters my secretary had placed there and with phone calls coming through. You were close to me, next to the radiator, sleeping or maybe pretending to sleep. Never failing, at 10.30 you put one of your little paws on my knee. I pretended not to notice, and after a while you put a second paw there. I still did not take notice and then, with a deep sigh, you pushed your little head through under my arm and looked straight into my face. "It's time to stop. Let's go out for a bit." This game became a daily occurrence. I am still missing it.

Another day I relive in my head is seeing you sitting in my car at the steering wheel, your eyes fixed on the door into the bank where I had gone. One day there were about ten people standing around the car and I almost had a heart attack seeing them all looking into it. I rushed across the street, expecting something terrible. But as soon as you saw me you jumped to your place on the old blanket on the back seat and assumed an air of innocence. You were not allowed in the front seats! I asked the people why they were standing there and they exclaimed "It was so damned cute seeing the little doggie with her paws on the steering wheel! But she never even looked at us, no matter what we did. Her eyes were fixed on the door across the street."

Oh yeah, Cindy, you were quite a character. When I came back from my annual trip to Europe after three weeks and my family was happy to see me, hugging me and finally, when looking at you, talking to you, you would walk away several steps, sit down and put your nose into the air, looking away from me. I admit, the first time this happened I was really hurt. But then, after a few hours, when the excitement of the family had died down, you came to me and showed me sooo much love, you

couldn't help yourself, wiggling, cuddling, making little noises-
oh my God, it brought tears to my eyes and I felt bad to have left
you for so long. I miss you to this very day.

It was the worst day in my life when I was called to the vet.
My seven year old boy Eric sat there crying, holding you on his
lap. You lifted your head just a bit, looked at me, giving a big
sigh as if to say: "I am so very sorry." Then the doc came,
carefully took you from Eric. You looked at me with very sad
eyes and after not even another minute doc came back and said:
"She is gone. Do you want to take her body or should we look
after it?"

Cindy, I cried for six weeks. You were my best friend. The
best I ever had. You gave me so much love, unconditional love,
during a time when my life was falling apart. Without you – I
honestly don't know what I would have done or how I would
have managed. This I have learned from you:

"TAKE MORE TIME."
    Just sitting there.
With big brown eyes you looked at me
to tell me - you are mine.
And I - pretend not seeing you
because
there was no time.
    Because there was no time?
You loved the car. You want to come?
One step - you stopped, then ran
you couldn't resist to be with me
One nod was all - oh man!
    When I lay down - you did that too
you were so close to me.

Oh little dog, where are you now -
I want you here, you see?
    I want you here. Just sitting there.
I'll tell you, you are mine.
I love you unconditionally
as you did all the time.
    It is too late. The car hit hard
your eyes, they closed forever.
    I'll never see your wagging tail
invite for play me, clever.
    It will be quiet in my house
no welcome bark nor whine -
Oh Cindy, why, oh Cindy why
did I not take more time.
    Did I not take more time...

26: I own this Joint

I liked the stamps from Liechtenstein best when I became interested in collecting postage stamps. Maybe they were not the most valuable but they were larger than postage stamps usually are and surely very pretty. I remember thinking each one of them looked like a painting.

Driving through picture perfect Switzerland with a friend in 1985 or maybe 1986, we decided on a side trip and pay a visit to Liechtenstein. Most people think Liechtenstein is part of Switzerland but it is not. Yes, they have a monetary union and share the Swiss franc but Liechtenstein is an independent monarchy bordered in the west and south by Switzerland and in the east and north by Austria. The history of the House of Liechtenstein with an unbroken heritage reads like a fairy tale. The Liechtenstein family is one of the oldest European noble families dating back to 1136. Originally they were connected to Austria but after a falling out one of the princes decided to have his own domain. In 1699 and later in 1712 the family purchased the county of Vaduz and the Dominion of Schellenberg. Those two were merged and through an Imperial Diploma by Charles VI declared the "Principality of Liechtenstein" in 1719.

The present Prince Hans-Adam von Liechtenstein is the 15th Prince to grow up in Vaduz, the capital. He was born in 1945 and through the House of Liechtenstein inheritance requirements has already passed on the reign to his son Alois, who now represents the country as Head of State. The Vaduz castle was built in the 12th century, burned, ransacked, rebuilt and extended over the hundreds of years owned by the 'House' and continues to serve as the main residence of the family. They lost incredibly large holdings of land and castles after WWII, annexed by the Russians and the Poles. They still own two palaces in the city of Vienna. One of them, the Palais of Liechtenstein, is open to cultural and art life in Vienna. We were invited to a concert and ballet performance when we were on the Budapest-Amsterdam River Cruise a few years ago.

The castle in Vaduz is the landmark of Liechtenstein, built on a very steep cliff overlooking the whole country. The population of Vaduz is a mere 5.500. The whole country measures only 160 square kilometers, it has eleven municipalities and a total population of 37.000. The largest city is Schaan. Vaduz is a very successful place of business. After WWII the principality suffered through a bad period and the family had to sell many treasures to survive. When they established international banking with many "letterbox" and "Trust companies", the country attracted the wealthiest international customers and now hosts more registered companies than citizens. The people of Liechtenstein enjoy one of the highest standards of living in the world. Personal income tax is merely 1.2% while business tax is around 12.5%. The unemployment rate is 1.5%. Banking, tourism, ceramic production (largest producer of artificial teeth in the world) and other industries provide more than enough income. Liechtenstein exports most of its electrical energy. And, let us not forget the wonderful stamps, collected everywhere.

During this first visit to Vaduz I bought two pairs of Bally shoes, the best shoes in the world. During our walking tour of the city we learned that the Prince was at home in his castle because a flag was raised. The castle is off limits for visitors but we could drive up the steep hill to a tourist parking lot and then wander through the natural surroundings, which we did. Actually, we could walk right up to the castle. A man in overalls was busy planting pansies. Several boxes with pansies, all the same pale blue colour were lined up next to him. After our greeting he stood up, took his worker gloves off and shook our hands. With him we looked at the beautiful view and he pointed out several interesting places, including an old church we shouldn't miss.

When parting, my friend said "You are lucky to work for the prince and be the gardener of such a beautiful place as these castle grounds.

"Oh no, sir, you are wrong. I own this joint."

27: It is Part of Ageing...

Elfie had her first cancer scare when she was in her forties. Something was wrong with her larynx. She had been a relatively heavy smoker since she was fairly young. Now the doctor told her to slow down. "Don't I have to stop?" she asked. "No" the good doctor advised her, "if you smoked twenty cigarettes up to now you can still smoke four or five a day."

How could a medical doctor tell a patient she may have cancer caused by her smoking and still allow her to smoke, even if it is less than usual? The story upset me and I told her:

"I think this man is irresponsible. If I were you I definitely would stop altogether. And find another doctor." Elfie said she would have no problem with stopping 'cold turkey' but she enjoys a cigarette.

"If my doctor says I can have a few, why should I stop?" A few months later we had another conversation. She had still smoked for a few more days but then quit because her symptoms got worse. It was cancer and she had to have a series of treatments.

Even now, years later, I find it difficult to figure out why the doctor had allowed her to smoke despite the obvious. Was it because he thought she couldn't stop anyway? The 'patch' had not been invented yet. People stopped because they wanted to stop, not because someone told them to stop. Elfie was lucky that the problem was diagnosed in time and before it had accelerated into a full blown cancer with dire consequences. As it happened she was a survivor. She never smoked again.

"I can taste my food. I had no idea I killed all those taste buds in my mouth. Everything had the same flavour, but now...it's great. I enjoy every bite."

Elfie and her family were living close to fine beaches and they enjoyed long summers in the sun in her very private garden. When the French people started to sunbath in the nude it didn't take long and "Nude Beach" signs were posted all along the beaches the family frequented. They became enthusiastic nudists. They were not the only ones. Families with children of all ages and grandparents, everybody lived life on the beach playing volley ball and running around as if still in the Garden of Eden. Every summer Elfie and her family were seamlessly tanned all over their bodies. They were, and looked, incredibly healthy and didn't mind that their faces had more leathery skin and deeper wrinkles. "It is part of ageing", Elfie said, laughing.

Years went by. We lost touch for a while and when I heard about Elfie again it was bad news. She had developed breast cancer and had a partial mastectomy. When our contact had been re-established she confided her story.

"We had bought an RV and were camping on a famous nude beach sixty kilometers from home. Gary and I were walking along the water, tiny waves just tickling our toes. It was a wonderful morning. I am still not sure but it must have been a fly I wanted to stroke off my breast when I felt this hard lump. I stopped and called "Gary, look, - what is this?" He claims he could see it without touching it. We packed up immediately and took off to get to an emergency hospital. The diagnosis was clear. Big C. I was devastated. They advised us to get home and check into the hospital. They had to operate, - right away. I had no choice."

A year later I heard from Elfie that she had had her left breast rebuilt out of her own flesh. She still wanted to look 'natural' on the nude beaches and not feel embarrassed. A few months later I telephoned and it was her husband Gary who answered the phone. He told me:

96

"Elfie is in the hospital to get her nipple re-done because the first one from a year ago fell off."

"What?" I couldn't help asking, - "How do they do that? Rebuild a nipple?"

He explained that the nipple is formed from a piece of flesh out of the vagina since it is the same kind of tissue. The breast had been rebuilt out of her buttock.

"Oh my God, why is she going through all that? There are so many people with mastectomies. They get bras fitted and look perfectly alright."

"For me, - she did not have to do all this" Gary replied, "I love her the way she is, nipple or not. But she still wants us to go to the nude beaches. She does not want to give that up. And she does not want people staring at her, especially not young children."

What a determined woman. She did not let the cancer get the better of her. She started eating organic food, explained to me that even the slightest spec of fungus on cheese is bad and she would discard the whole piece; she is still enjoying the sun but with a higher sun protection factor. They spend every winter in Spain or Morocco meeting other RV friends and enjoy life to the fullest. She does not think of being old or looking old or ageing, looks don't matter to Elfie. She is now seventy but very positive, loves her very supportive husband and her grown up children and grandchildren. It is ten years since her operation and she is cancer free.

A survivor.

28: Desperately Wanted: A Baby

Heavy tears rolled down Emma's face. The letter in her hands was already wet and her mind still couldn't wrap itself around the fate which had befallen her niece Jenny. There had been no intimate communication for many years, just the usual birthday and Christmas cards across two continents. Now this letter! Out of the blue a story fit for Readers Digest magazine.

Jenny, quite young and much in love with Rodney, a year younger than she, expected a baby. They married but could not find a place of their own. Rodney's parents let them live in his boyhood room while both worked. Jenny's baby was born by Caesarian section. She developed childbed fever while in the hospital, a complication hardly known in modern times. Fighting for her life for six weeks and only semiconscious, Jenny's mother, a pediatric nurse, insisted on surgery and the doctors finally agreed to open her up again. They found a wad of cotton and scissors in her abdomen. The outlook was dismal. A total hysterectomy was necessary to save her life. Jenny was nineteen years old. The baby boy Cory was the joy for all, the young couple and the grandparents on both sides. Cory had the happiest childhood.

"Dear Aunt Emma, our Cory is gone. We wished so much for another child over the years but I could not have any. I was often afraid Rodney would leave me, being such a family man. Our Cory was everything to us. He was a good teenager, never in trouble and now he is gone, gone forever. A careless driver backing out of a parking place when Cory was passing him on his bicycle with another boy riding pillion sent them both flying. Cory hit his head on a tree, the other boy got away with just scraped knees and arms. Cory was unconscious and when we finally got to see him we had to make a heart wrenching decision: Let him live as a vegetable, never regaining consciousness or pull the plug."

Emma was staring at the letter with unseeing eyes. She couldn't believe how much her young niece had gone through but there was more. Jenny and Rodney had never been christened, confirmed or married in the church. Cory therefore had not been christened either. Religion was frowned upon in communist East Germany where they lived. It hit them hard when the pastor of the church in their village said "NO" to their son's funeral service and burial in the church yard. They checked with the church in the neighbouring village. It was the same there: "You have never been to our services." They checked a third village with a female pastor who agreed to conduct a funeral service if they promised to take a three months course, get christened themselves and become regular church goers. They agreed and the church became a saviour in their grief.

"My God," Emma thought, "is that what Christians do nowadays?"

The next request shocked Emma even more if that was possible. They couldn't live without a child. They had tried the local adoption agency. Their home checked out fine but they, at 35 and 36 were too old to adopt a baby. They were devastated. They were depressed and anxious.

"Aunty, you are a woman of the world, please can you help us find a surrogate mother in your country? It's not allowed here. We are willing to put all our savings into this. Rodney is a healthy man and he is willing to do whatever it takes. Artificial insemination or otherwise and I am totally on board. Please, please, help us. But please do not tell my parents, they will not understand. Please keep this between us. We'll understand if you turn us down or if you never answer this letter."

100

Finally Emma got up, made herself a cup of tea and stood a long time looking out of her window. How could she answer a desperate letter like this? How to answer this despairing cry for help? The faith her niece put in her? She had always thought of Jenny as a long legged model, someone like the English "Twiggy". Emma considered her niece even prettier but without the prospects of Twiggy. Never in her wildest dreams would she have thought of tragedies like this in Jenny's life. Her love, her loss and her desperate wish to be a mother again... How tragic losing her only son and not being able to bear another child because of the carelessness of the surgical team when she had the Caesarian section at nineteen years of age.

"Okay, no matter what", Emma said to herself, "I have to give her my honest opinion. It's not even a year since Cory died; the grieving process takes much longer." Resolutely she put her tea cup down on her desk. Pen in hand she pulled the paper closer and after expressing her overwhelming shock on receiving the letter she counselled Jenny to give her mind and body more time to adjust to the loss of Cory.

"Don't try to replace him because it can never be done. Find and join a grief support group. Think of the responsibilities a new baby will bring into your life when you are still in shock and under such heavy psychological stress.

"Jenny, my dear girl, you know what I think is the best for now? To help you find peace with yourself again? Get a dog, or a cat. A little pet will give you responsibility, it needs your love and attention, and you will get its love a thousand fold in return. As for finding a surrogate mother, there are terrible dangers. A recent case reported on our television here involved a mother of four children. To earn extra money her husband had agreed to let her be the surrogate mother for a childless couple, desperate for a baby. They received a huge amount of money, more than the husband would make in a year. The baby was born, the happy couple came to pick it up but the surrogate mother could not bear to give it up and decided to keep it. The childless couple went to court. The court awarded the baby to the woman who had carried it for nine months and loved it. The cheated couple even has to pay child support. No, my dear, this is not the way to go. It sounds terrible but it might be better if your husband would have an affair with a woman who might in the end let him raise a joint child."

Emma added a few more sentences to the letter to round it off and promised to never speak to anyone about this correspondence. "Cry on my shoulder, dear Jenny, keep in touch, write to me, it will be just between you and me."

Several months later the next letter arrived. "We have a cat already", Jenny wrote, "and we don't want a dog." The pain did not seem quite as raw and the suggestion of the grief support group had taken hold. Jenny had received psychiatric treatment in the hospital where she had spent several weeks.

"At first I just cried during the group sessions", Jenny wrote, "but some of the stories the other parents told made me realize I wasn't the only one carrying such a heavy burden. My Cory probably didn't even realize what hit him, it all went so fast. But some of these people talk of childhood cancer, terrible mental problems with children nearly grown up and no help available, children having lost limbs or turned blind because of fires.

"Aunt Emma, I still want a baby. The leader of the group sessions is also in charge of an adoption agency. She is very nice to me. She has promised to let me know should there be a baby available. We would have to be quick to react if we get a call. We are turning Cory's room into a baby room and pray God hears us. The lady pastor in our church has the whole congregation praying for us. If anything good has come out of Cory's death it was finding this church. I don't know how we would have been able to get through the worst time with thoughts of suicide. Now we have an extended family. My parents think we have gone crazy. They will never understand."

Emma suggested volunteering in an orphanage to find a child, a child she would be drawn to and vice versa. She tried to be loving and supportive, but continued to point out the pros and cons of an adoption and how important it is to know where a baby comes from including the history of its parents regarding future health issues. Jenny dismissed all Emma's thoughts with determination to have a new baby in her life.

Another very happy and ecstatic letter announced the birth of little Billy. He was only a couple of days old when they got the call. A baby boy was available. The mother didn't want him. She had three children, the oldest already twenty-one, the youngest ten years old. Rodney and Jenny were the happiest couple on earth when they picked up their baby from the hospital and brought him home into Cory's room.

Baby Billy cried a lot. He didn't even take a soother or the bottle, he cried and cried. Only Rodney could get him somewhat settled in his arms, calm him and feed him. The baby totally rejected Jenny. She had another breakdown, was hospitalized again and Rodney took time off work to care for little Billy. When Jenny came home they took Billy to their doctor. The baby was referred to a specialist at the University. The final testing result was another shock: Billy had fetal alcohol withdrawal symptoms. Rodney spoke to the adoption agency. He was told the mother was an alcoholic, was hugely obese, had not realized she was pregnant and had given birth to the baby sitting on the toilet. The child had dropped in, head first. Her oldest son had come home, heard the commotion in the bathroom and was just in time to rescue the baby. He phoned for a taxi and took both, mother and baby to the hospital. Rodney and Jenny were horrified when they heard this story and now understood why nobody else had wanted to adopt this baby. They had not been told any of this before the adoption.

Another heart wrenching letter to her aunt seemed Jenny's only relief. "What am I to do? I cannot handle the baby, he screams when I touch him; only Rodney can calm him. Aunt Emma, I am losing my mind."

Emma remained realistic: "The baby will always be a problem. Can't you give him back to be cared for in a special institution?"

The answer she received shouldn't have surprised her:

"We wanted a baby. God heard our cries and gave us this baby. We had him christened. If I had given birth to him I would also keep him. No, Aunt Emma, we cannot give him back."

This was one of the last letters for years. Emma learned from Jenny's mother little Billy had been an ongoing problem, sometimes behaving like a dog, running up to and biting people. "He has developed so much strength that he rips doors out of their frame and breaks windows. He needs to go to a special school with an attendant sitting next to him at all times.

"The only way to handle him is with medication. It has side effects but without it we cannot control him. Even if Jenny is late a few minutes in giving it to him he causes trouble. We all hope he grows out of it in time."

Is there a moral to this story? It's hard to say. Jenny has stopped writing to Emma.

29: Spring – The Ice Was Starting to Melt...

Avril was sitting on the steps of her daughter's country house on a thick pillow with a shawl wrapped over her shoulders. She watched her grandsons slide back and forth over the ice still covering most of the puddles in the yard. The ice was starting to melt at the edges, but the center was still strong enough to hold the small bodies. She smiled as the kiddies were intent on breaking the ice with their boots, stamping on it. They were screaming with joy when they hit water and did not stop until all the ice was broken up and the pieces were lying around like shards of glass. They jumped up and down in the water until it was all dispersed and after one puddle they moved on to the next. Memories assaulted Avril as she thought of herself as a child at about the same age as the oldest boy.

She had been totally deaf since she was ten years old. She lost her hearing during "The Blitz" in WWII. A direct hit had killed most of the people in a public shelter in London. Her parents were killed. Miraculously she was one of the very few survivors, but now orphaned. She was running along the road with strangers during the ongoing bombing. The noise was deafening and her ear drums had burst. A couple of Air Raid wardens picked her up and made sure she was united with her uncle living on an estate on the outskirts of London. He became her guardian and she lived with his family until she became an adult. People who did not know about her handicap would never have guessed. She had learned to lip-read and was incredibly good at it.

"Oh God", she thought with a deep sigh, "Please, let these kiddies never experience a war. But despite it all, I had an interesting life. Have I really lived more than eighty years? It all went so fast..." She shook her white head.

Avril had been a very beautiful sixteen year old girl when a movie company offered her a part. She wanted to accept but her guardian uncle did not permit it. He reminded her of her family status coming from an old aristocratic family. She had argued the old times were over and what did it matter now if she was related to King George, six times removed? At sixteen, just like all girls, she could hardly wait to grow up and be independent. She studied fashion and did some modelling. At the ripe old age of twenty-two she accepted a job offer from a designer company. After a few years working in the UK she was sent to Canada to introduce their designs and some of her own in the rapidly growing cities of Montreal, Toronto and Vancouver. She organized successful fashion shows. Since she was curious about and intrigued by life in British Columbia she accepted the invitation of new friends and accompanied them to Powell River, north of Vancouver for a short holiday.

"By golly – what luck that was", she smiled as she was sitting on the steps, and, her eyes, not focussing on the kids anymore, looked into the distance and she saw it all happen again. She had met Jack, a young dentist, at a dance. He hailed from Vancouver but his first job had to be outside of the big city. It was love at first sight. Both liked hiking. They explored the area around Powel River and not always stayed on marked trails. Watching her grandchildren play on the ice reminded her of one of their hikes. They had walked for hours and had wanted to cut off part of the miles on their way home. A frozen river with a fallen tree about five meters above the ice presented a problem. They discussed if they should try to walk across it or walk further along downriver and hope it might narrow so they could then cross it. Avril had decided to use the tree while Jack opted for the alternative. A smile curled Avril's lips as she thought of them walking on opposite sides of the river. It seemed like yesterday.

"Jack, my dear Jack! How could a strong man like you be afraid of heights? That tree was perfect! If you couldn't walk you could have crawled across it."

The ice had started to melt at the shallow edges. It didn't seem to be a fast flowing river and the ice still seemed quite strong. Jack had contemplated on turning back but then they indeed came to a narrower part where the river squeezed through a rock formation. The ice was piled up and looked solid. Jack carefully stepped on it and it held. So step by careful step he inched towards the middle when he heard the cracking sound. Avril's world was quiet but she saw Jack's arm movements and lip read the words he uttered and knew he was in trouble. There was no turning back. The next step forward placed him knee deep into the ice cold water. Lifting one foot to get back up on the ice just broke more of it.

Avril re-lived the scene.

When he was close enough he accepted my hand and I helped him to get up onto the rocks. He sat down to take his wet hiking boots and socks off and tried to squeeze as much water as he could from his trousers. I offered my warm scarf and he tore it in half to wrap his feet in it and then he put the wet boots back on. After about half an hour of climbing a hill he stopped, faced me and exclaimed:

"Avril, I think I discovered a new treatment. My feet have never felt this incredible warmth! Either it's because of your scarf or it was the ice cold water...Will you marry me?"

The memory lit up Avril's face, - and she said aloud: "Yes"

One of her grandsons stood in front of her and asked,

"Grandma?" Her mind was immediately back in the present and looking at the boy she added,

"Yes, - the ice is definitely starting to melt…"

30: A Beautiful Rose for a Beautiful Lady

It was a small airport somewhere along the Greek coast. A bus was waiting to deliver all the guests to their respective hotels. Looking towards the back of the bus I noticed that everybody seemed to come in "twos": couples, two women or even two men. One glimpse and I was surprised to see the second row wasn't taken. I sat down by the window. I was used to traveling by myself in Europe after the conclusion of my business. Greece had always intrigued me and last year I had enjoyed a "Classic Greek Tour" by bus and saw all the famous sites, even learned about the 'Delphi oracle.' This time I wanted a week at a sunny beach.

As more people entered the bus I wondered what kind of seat neighbour I would get. Could it be "the one"? Tall, dark and handsome? You never know, right? More twosomes pushed by and finally a middle aged woman asked "Is this seat taken?"

"Now it is." I smiled at her, pointing to the seat. She had an easy laugh and sat down. It didn't take long and I knew her life story. She wanted to know at which hotel along the strip I had booked. It happened to be the very last one, two stops after she had to get out. Her hotel looked pretty nice; it had a beautiful driveway up to the main entrance through a gorgeous garden. Small black and white pebbles, apparently laid by hand, formed intricate designs. I was impressed and hoped my hotel would be this nice. Marianne disembarked with "Bye, I'll visit you soon."

Well, my hotel was just as nice as the picture had been in the travel catalogue. The receptionist was incredibly friendly. I loved my room overlooking the swimming pool and the Mediterranean. It actually was a five star hotel while Marianne's had only three stars. The beach was a bit disappointing. There was no sand, just millions of pebbles and little rocks washed smooth by the rolling waves. I had to buy a pair of plastic sandals to wear when I wanted to go swimming. The hotel had lots of German guests. I had been placed at a table with an elderly couple from Hamburg. We were chatting over an afternoon drink when Marianne turned up. She found us, just took a seat and exclaimed: "This is heaven! I don't have access to the sea. I think I'll visit you every day!" Open and outspoken as she was it did not take long and the Hamburgers knew she was from Kiel in Holstein and was looking for an apartment in Hamburg. She was going to start a new job there after her holiday. It turned out my new Hamburger friends knew of an apartment in their building and after a phone call to the manager Marianne had rented it. Wow! Talk about coincidences and luck!

After a small lull in our conversation with Marianne being the main contributor she told us about her arrival in her hotel. All had gone well. She had a nice room on the main floor with a double bed and she joked about a recent stay in a psychiatric clinic. She had needed help after a really lousy painful divorce. The double bed had reminded her and she fled the room and took a walk through the gardens. She noticed lots of roses in one area. "I went closer to smell the roses", she told us, "and I was a bit shocked when a deep voice from behind a huge specimen said 'hello'. A tanned, handsome man was dead-heading the roses and she took him to be the gardener. "You won't believe it", she told us with, by now, really rosy cheeks, "When I found my voice again I complimented him on the beautiful garden and told him I loved roses. He took a branch with a gorgeous rose on it, clipped it off and handed it to me with the words,

"A beautiful rose for a beautiful lady".

We were impressed, laughed and talked about the charm of the Greeks. She came back the next day for a swim and we again had our nice little table in the shady corner.

"You won't believe what I have to tell you today! Last night after dinner I was writing in my diary. There was a knock on the door. I went to open it and a waiter stood there, carrying a tray with a bottle of wine in an ice bucket, two glasses and a rose. I told him he must be at the wrong door because I did not order anything. He had a note and was adamant mine was the right room. He simply walked in and set down the tray on a small table in front of the window. He left and closed the door behind him. I

 did not know what to make of it and was afraid to go to bed. I would have loved to drink a glass of wine. I had the suspicion the gardener had sent it but since there were two glasses I didn't dare to start the bottle. I got tired of waiting

so, as it was close to midnight, got myself ready for bed and sat there in the dark expecting a knock on the door at any time. But it didn't happen. Finally I slipped down under the blanket and drifted off to sleep.

"Can you believe this? What would you have done? I never was so unsure, anxious and even a bit afraid in my whole life. I am not sure what I would have done had he turned up. At breakfast this morning I saw a well-dressed man walk through the room, greeting every guest at every table and finally he came to mine. Can you imagine my shock? It was the gardener! And he was no gardener, he was the manager! I was totally flabbergasted. He asked me if I enjoyed the wine. I told him I had thought it wasn't for me and since there were two glasses I didn't dare drink it but I had realized it must be from him and I had thought of him all night."

"That was the idea, my lady" he said. He gave me the biggest smile and bowed before moving on to the next table."

Wow! What an idea! Who else but a charming Greek man can come up with such an idea?

31: "May Day, May Day"

May Day is a traditional holiday in several European countries but for me the intriguing part is what leads up to it in Bavaria.

A few weeks before the first of May the young males of every village go scouting for the straightest and tallest tree in the surrounding forests. Once they find "the one" they have to guard it to avoid it being claimed by the young men from another rival village. Before anybody can cut any tree they need permission from the Forestry Commission to cut it down and bring it home. Once permission is granted the tree is marked. Now the dangerous game of protecting your own tree and trying to steal another marked for another village is in full swing. The young men of every village, and there are many villages every few kilometers, get involved and they are busy every night with the protection of "their tree" because attempts to succeed are made by every single one. Why? If one village or another succeeds in 'stealing' a tree the loser has to pay for all the beer they will drink during that year whenever there is a chance. I wonder how much beer is already consumed during the cold nights protecting their prospective tree!

The tree has to be cut and brought home in the old fashioned way, no machinery allowed. It also has to be erected without any help of modern conveniences. Ropes and muscle power is what's needed. The bark is removed in a certain way to leave a design according to tradition in the particular village. Once the tree is "up" a wreath, called a "crown", is hung at the highest possible spot, often they even attach another small tree on top to reach an even greater height. May poles eighty or even hundred metres high are not rare. All the way down from the top carved logo signs from every profession in the village or town are attached. I gather those professions, be it tailor, shoemaker, farmer, hotelier or even the church have to pay to have their painted carvings depicting the profession on the 'May Pole'. And they are proud to do so! Most villagers get involved in the erection of the pole and especially in the celebrations during and after they have completed the task. Since it is hard work without any mechanical help the men get very thirsty and again lots of beer will find its way into thirsty throats. Usually there is a brewery in the village or close by. They have a fresh brew, the 'May Brew' ready which surely needs to be tested as well. After the 'May Pole' is proudly standing and secured the people hurry home because now they have to prepare for another happening.

April the 30th is 'Walpurgis Night'. It's an anxious and frightening night for all the villagers. It is the night when all the witches are loose. They do some crazy things and no one stops them. One year I happened to be in the beautiful Bavarian health resort of Bad Wörishofen and my hosts were taking all their lawn chairs, terrace furniture and garden ornaments into their hallway. Questioned, they explained to me these items could end up in a totally different part of the city or even hidden in places you wouldn't think of looking for them, in some cases overturned or broken. Police? Forget it. After all, the police do not deal with 'witches'. It's free rein to do mischief without being punished. Mostly it's all done in good fun.

During breakfast next morning we had a really good laugh because something "new", never done before, had happened. All the street signs were covered and new names making fun of certain officials or happenings in the village were placed on top. The one most people got a big kick out of was "Roter Platz" (Red Square) at the centre surrounding the statue of Father Kneipp, the "Water Doctor", a priest who had made this city famous during the 19th century. (As a matter of fact, at least 95% of the population still make their living catering to the "Water Kur" guests.) This plaza had recently been tiled with red tiles and the former grass and the flower beds had been removed. The old-timers in the city didn't like the transformation. The prank with the "Red Square" did not go over too well with the Mayor's office. However, the old street names were restored within a few hours.

The first of May is a big holiday. Literally everybody has been praying for sunshine and, with luck, the weatherman has listened. People gather in their old fashioned costumes around the "Kurhaus", the bands tune their instruments and a parade winds its way throughout the city aiming to end the march at the May Pole. There are lots of stalls with bratwurst, pretzels and beer (of course!), herring buns, home-made torts and cakes hosted by the different women's groups. There is coffee, ice cream, sugar puffs and drinks for the children and more beer for the ones who happened to be lucky enough to find a seat for the rest of the day. The bands play their catchy tunes, the folk dancers as young as two years or as old as ninety congregate around the May Pole and do their infectious dances. Lots and lots of cameras click to catch the excitement. When the official part is over the pubs fill up and the new fresh "Maybock" beer, a strong brew, leads to the downfall of many a drinker who overestimated

115

their capacity to "hold their beer". But May Day is fun, it's so much fun! If you ever have a chance to experience it, - rather than aiming for a big city, try to find a smaller village and mingle with the 'natives'. And be sure not to overestimate your capacity when sampling the "Maybock"!

I was told that many a maiden would have called "May Day - May Day" if she would have been aware of the happenings on May Day when she found herself "in the family way" a few weeks after.

32: "Blue Hawaiian"...Hula and Aloha

Is there anybody out there who has NOT dreamed about going to Hawaii at least once? The TV series "Hawaii 5-0" and many movies filmed on these beautiful islands with some of the highest mountains in the world (measured from the ocean floor), the many waterfalls and, for the history buff, the books about Captain Cook and Pearl Harbour have inspired generations. They still do. Ten of the most beautiful beaches in the world, the highest waves attracting world class surfers, the infamous 'Road to Hana', the drive up to Haleakala to see the most incredible sunrise and the rare silver thistle growing up there in the freezing cold, the active volcano Kilauea, the pineapple fields, the pleasant climate and last but not least, the romantic music and the Hula dancers attract millions of visitors year round.

The island of Maui has become my favourite after probably fifteen visits to the other known Hawaiian Islands. The Ka'anapali Beach Hotel is our 'home away from home Why the Ka'anapali Beach Hotel? It is the most Hawaiian of all the Hawaiian hotels, employing Hawaiians with a team spirit which lets the visitor wonder who is actually in charge.

Malihini, a woman with an almost visible aura of love sits at the reception desk. She is a descendent of a very old Polynesian family. She carries on the knowledge in native medicine; she dances and explains the hula movements, teaches the Hawaiian language and is involved in everything "truly Hawaiian".

Everyone is greeted with "Aloha". It means many things: Love, compassion, affection, good wishes, hello, good bye and many more. The hugs you receive when coming back show you that you are part of the 'Ohana', - the Hawaiian family. At the end of your first holiday you receive a dark kukui nut lei (necklace), and each time you come back a pale beige kukui nut replaces a black one. Count the beige nuts, add one year and you know how often a guest wearing the lei has visited. Since the employees wear the leis as well you wonder why so many have only light nuts around their neck. Those who do have been working there for 25 years and longer, no room anymore for black nuts! The best thing about KBH along the famous Ka'anapali Beach with international hotels like the Westin, Hyatt, Sheraton, Marriott, Hilton and many others is the very large green space with old trees, providing privacy and choice to tan in the sun or rest in the shade. It's very unlike the other hotels where beach chairs are lined up side by side with no room between them. KBH offers free daily activities like cultural garden walks, pineapple cutting, Hawaiian language instruction, lei making from flowers or leaves, leaf weaving, kiddies programs, ukulele lessons, singing, storytelling and last, but not least, hula dancing, which, next to the language lessons, is my favourite.

Naturally the grounds of KBH face onto the beach. The delight of all morning joggers is the approximately two kilometer long beach walk. It remains busy all day. Groups of people staring out to sea are watching the whales playing, jumping, blowing and waving their tail greetings. Whale watching tours bring you close to the whales jumping or blowing right next to the boat, dive under and around it and could easily push it over since they are much bigger than the boats. I never am totally at ease and can't overcome the feeling it could happen. But I have never heard of anybody who ever experienced it.

Did you know the Hawaiian language has only five vowels and seven consonants in their alphabet? That's why many words seem to be doubled up i.e. Kamehameha or "Humu humu nuku nuku apua'a", - the name of the Hawaiian Statefish! There was a time when I wished I could move to Hawaii. I wanted to learn the old language and the hula, and, after mastering it, teach both to tourists. Mainlanders who have opened businesses on the islands warned me about "Island fever". They are allowed to fly to the mainland every so often on a low fare in order not to fall victim to this secretive but apparently devastating "dis-ease". I dream on and leave it to always enjoyable holidays.

"Aloha"!

33: One More Try and You'll Make It...

My friend Ursula suggested a holiday and fly to Hawaii for a week or two. We both owned our own businesses and it wasn't always easy to get away. I had a secretary who was capable of looking after my wholesale company. Ursula was not sure if she could leave her only assistant, who had just recently finished her esthetician training, alone. In the end she decided it was a slow time anyway and if she lost some money, so be it. She needed a break.

We stayed a few days in Honolulu, enjoyed the beautiful beach during the day and enjoyed a sunset drink under the huge Banyan Tree of the "Old Moana Hotel". It took us only a couple of days to forget our world at home. The Hawaiian music combined with the slow movements of the Hula dancers during 'Happy Hour' lifted our spirits and took us on a different kind of journey as we were watching the sun sink into the ocean.

"Ursula, - watch it, - look for the green flash!" I reminded her. We had tried several times to see it but it never happened for her. I saw it once. It happens at the very last moment, the moment when the last bit of sun finally slips into the water. My eyes hurt from staring. I wonder how a scientist would explain this magical happening to the Polynesians. The "green flash" is special wherever in the world it happens.

One evening we wandered through the "International Market". We found a great restaurant and frequented it a few more times. The most exciting thing was looking at all the colourful beach wear and the mumus, 'designed' by the first missionaries for the happily naked Hawaiians. We admired the many wonderful booths' with jewellery, we tried our hand at picking an oyster out of a basket, watched the attendant knock on it and then open it to find either a black, a grey or a white pearl inside it. It is incredible how an oyster can make such beautiful pearls just because something irritates it. The Hawaiian sales clerk always tries to sell you either a ring or a pendant to set your new treasure, or entice you to pay for and pick another oyster to make it a pair of earrings. They promise to get you the same color. How could they know that? They just smile their magic secretive Hawaiian smile. We watched them long enough to see the sale of two oysters to another tourist. The sales clerk did pick an oyster with a second pearl of the same color. How did she know? The shells looked all the same.

The best and most exciting evening was when we discovered a Tarot card reader behind a huge big tree. We were listening and watching the proceedings. After debating if it was worth the money we decided to go ahead. This Psychic knew nothing about us. We were not going to tell her anything and, we figured, it's just a bit of fun. Little did we anticipate to being overwhelmed by the result. She, or the cards we had to pick, revealed so much of our past and present we were convinced that the future prognosis was right too.

Ursula was divorced and as part of the settlement she had the right to spend two weeks a year in her former husband's townhouse on the isle of Molokai. Once upon a time the people with Leprosy, the "Lepers" had been sent to this isle. Molokai does not have fine beaches. Close to where we were staying was just a small stretch of beach. Once you stepped off the beach you were in deep water. Ursula never went in, I did. I love to swim in the soft salty water. It feels like silk against my skin. Once I had to call on Ursula:

"I can't get out! Please come and help me!"

Ursula came, knelt down and said:

"Here, Giselle, hold onto my hand" and she pulled. I held on but she slipped and also ended up in the water. Thank goodness she could swim. She had swallowed some water and was a bit frantic. I had to push her up to the beach and in the end I found a spot where I could heave myself out as well.

We had this little beach all to ourselves. We pushed some sand up and made a shallow bowl to lie down without our tops on. If you have never sunbathed in the nude you don't know the incredible feeling of freedom. The beach was bordered by a strip of no-mans-land with lots of shrubs and bushes and a few large trees and beyond it was a golf course. While we were dozing and enjoying the sun I heard some careful steps on the dry leaves in the bushes behind us:

"Hey, - Ursula, - hear that?"

"God, those old turkeys! Why would they need to sneak up on us? Have they never seen girls without tops? Maybe they look for lost balls..."

Both of us were quick to cover ourselves. When we looked around, safely clad in our bathing suits, we could not see any one. Suddenly Ursula exclaimed:

"For heaven's sakes! Those are real turkeys. Look over there! I forgot to tell you there are lots of wild turkeys on Molokai!" We had a good laugh and took our tops off again.

Naturally I wanted to see the Lepers colony or, more like it, what was left of it. We joined a guided tour and the young Polynesian knew how to tell a story. The poor people afflicted with leprosy were simply dropped off from a boat, never to see their families again. Another boat would come once a week to off-load food and drinking water and maybe letters from loved ones. The boat always left in a hurry. The lepers had to fend for themselves until they died. A good soul named Father Damien had come and stayed and helped them to build little houses, a makeshift hospital for their last days and a small church. They lived life one day at a time while a nose, a finger or a toe fell off. There was no stopping it. I was shaken by this horrible affliction and the inhuman way the poor people had to live out their life. It was the best the Hawaiians or the missionaries could do at the time to protect the rest of their families. Some loving wives would accompany their husbands and help Father Damien to care for the ones in the small hospital. In the end they and Father Damien caught the disease and died there as well.

We had come the long way, walking through a forest. On the way back we wanted to make it quicker and decided to climb up the rope ladder attached to a very high, steep cliff. A few couples who were on the tour with us joined us. We two women went first, and not even halfway up I had to keep saying to myself: "Keep on going, - you can do this".

I had not counted on the strength it took to pull your weight up a ladder going straight up to heaven. Ursula, less sportive than I and with a few more pounds on her frame, really had trouble. One of the men behind her warned her and asked permission which was not withheld:

"Lady, I can push, but I'll have to touch your bum, sorry about that but it's the only way. Come on, - one more try, keep on going, you'll make it!" Once arrived at the top she fell flat on her face, exhausted. I sat next to her to recover. We were also emotionally exhausted. It had not been easy to see the place and hear the story so well told by the guide, it had been heart wrenching. But we had made it up the steep climb.

We enjoyed the little beach for a few more days. Actually we were glad to get back to the hustle and bustle of Honolulu.

34: Flying On Points...

"It's a miserable, humdrum life, and I have had enough of it".

Betty and Jim were coming back from their honeymoon and had just boarded flight 101 moments earlier after an exciting week on the Hawaiian Island of Maui. They looked forward to starting their life as a married couple and wanted to share happiness, not misery. Betty was disappointed they had to sit next to a miserable old coot. The man seemed destined to spoil what had been such a wonderful vacation.

"Miserable? Humdrum? What has happened to put you in such despair?" Happy new husband Jim asked.

"It's just everything. I've lost a lot of money on a fund I was talked into by a sleek con-man. My wife is mad at me because I had not talked it over with her before I invested. She was furious and was screaming at me calling me all kinds of names. I lost my job because I couldn't concentrate anymore. She might lose her little farm because I had mortgaged it to get more money to invest and get rich quick. I did it for her. She is a hard worker. I wanted to give her a better life, at least take her on an extended holiday. When she found out what I had done she threw me out. Up to now I have lived in a basement room and tried to make it on the little I earned by selling vacuum cleaners door to door, - the new kind, you know, the ones using water. Sometimes people close the door in my face and a few times I was just pushed out the door by the husband when a wife got too interested. It's a miserable, humdrum life. So, there you have it."

Jim looked at Betty, lifted his left shoulder a bit as was his habit when he didn't know what to say. They settled into their seats, put the seat belts on and waited for the airplane to take off.

Betty had the window and Jim the middle seat, the aisle was taken up by Mr. Humdrum. That practically made them his prisoners. They would have to ask him to get up when they needed to stretch their legs or go to the restroom. However, they were newlyweds, had entwined their hands and Betty had put her head on her husband's shoulder. Both looked out of the window. Betty was repeatedly kicked in the back by a kid sitting behind her. She turned around and gave the mother an angry look who spoke to the young boy in a different language and for a while the kicking stopped.

The flight attendant came through to make sure everybody had their seatbelt on and the backrest up. When she came to the aisle seat in the bulk head row the back of the chair would not stay upright. She apologized to the white haired gentleman sitting there and told him someone would come to check the seat. Another flight attendant went through the usual exercise with the explanations about the seatbelts, the drop of the oxygen masks and the emergency procedures. Finally a male steward came to check the seat. He couldn't make it stay in position either. He offered to move the gentleman to another seat farther back. Mr. Humdrum, Betty and Jim were in the fourth row. The elderly gentleman refused to move unless he was upgraded into business class with his wife. The steward was very polite, explained the flight was fully booked with the exception of a couple of seats in the same cabin. His wife could move there with him. A strict refusal in an angry tone was the answer. The steward left but soon came back with the purser, a beautiful lady with a soft voice. Her manners were impeccable. She was emphatic, stating because of strict regulations the airplane would not be able to take off and for safety reasons the seat has to be vacated. By now everybody within earshot was quiet and listened to an angry exchange. Betty and Jim were incredulous because the purser and the steward never lost their cool and were extremely polite. Mr. Humdrum whispered: "If that would be me, I would throw the old bugger out of the plane."

He wasn't so far off. Two security men entered and with them came a technician. He tried to fix the seat, finally shook his head and said "Sorry, the seat has to be replaced. It cannot be done now since the airplane is scheduled to take off and we don't have another one to replace it." He left and the security men asked the gentleman to either move or they would have to take him off the plane. By now, the flight was already thirty minutes late.

"Do you know who you are talking to? I have thirteen members of my family sitting in the rows around me. We are all flying on points. I am your most frequent flyer. I still have more than a million points on your airline and I will not move unless you upgrade my wife and me. I will not get off this airplane. I am staying in this seat no matter what you say about safety or security rules."

Finally, the security men left. Flight 101 was grounded. The captain announced he was sorry for the delay but not able to take off until "a security matter" was resolved. The people all around us got restless and some of them expressed their sentiments. "Wonder why he is flying economy if he has so many points…" - "He puts all of us in danger by not obeying the safety rules" – "What a gall…" – "Does he think he owns the airline?" –"Seems to be a rich bugger from…" - "Be careful what you say, he may sue you for discrimination" – and Mr. Humdrum expressed his thoughts with "You'll see, he'll get away with it because he is such a frequent flyer. You or I, we wouldn't." All these words were spoken kind of 'under the breath' but in the quiet cabin everyone could hear them.

Betty was getting the kicks in her back again. The little boy got restless. Who could blame him? Everybody was restless. Betty turned, looked at the boy and said, "Please, stop that, it hurts you know." Another boy of about twelve or thirteen sat next to him. He said something to the lady and she put the young one on the floor in the aisle next to her. He became a holy terror to a lot of people. Everybody realized he belonged to the big family with their million flight points grandfather and put up with it.

After more than an hour the captain spoke again, apologized for the long delay and announced he would be starting within the next ten minutes. Finally, the flight was on its way.

"What did I tell you?" Mr. Humdrum was in a totally different mood. "The seat is not fixed, the man did not move. I wonder if the captain took the responsibility for it or the airline authorities are afraid they would lose a frequent flyer. Maybe he even does own the airline or lots of shares."

Mr. Humdrum actually became an interesting conversation partner. He was well read, was politically up-to-date and quite an extrovert with a terrific sense of humour. The hours of the flight went by rather quickly.

After the touchdown in Vancouver the captain asked the passengers to let people with tight connections deplane first. The big family did not listen. They got up and stood in the isle and nobody could get through. They were also blocking the way walking four or five abreast as everybody headed towards the luggage carousel. They all crowded around the old gentleman, talked animatedly to him and seemed quite proud he had stood his ground. Mr. Humdrum stayed with Betty and Jim until they had their luggage and had to hurry to catch their connecting flight. Mr. Humdrum had made up his mind about his wife. He would phone her, explain where he was, tell her he intended to look for a job in the big city or, if she agrees, he would come home to her and try to get his old job back. By now he knew Betty and Jim were newlyweds and very much appreciated they had encouraged him not to give up.

"Let me tell you a joke", Mr. Humdrum offered before they parted.

"A couple in their late thirties got married. They went on their honeymoon booked in a beautiful hotel. The first morning the husband came to the restaurant by himself and ordered a huge breakfast. The waiter inquired,

"Sir, is your wife going to join you?"

"Oh," the husband said happily, "she is sleeping in and will come down later."

The waiter stood at the door and kept an eye on his guests. He happened to look at the large curved stairway when he saw a woman holding onto the railing as she came down, one step at a time. He hurried towards her and asked:

"Are you alright? Can I help you?"

The woman just shook her head:

"I am alright. It's just – well, my husband had always told me he had been saving up all his life. And I thought - he - meant money…"

Mr. Humdrum laughed, "Have a safe trip home, folks!"

35: The House is Empty....

The train was rolling along through almost flat lands, - home, home to Gary's hometown in the Mid-West. It was two years since he had left, not because he wanted to but he had been conscripted to fight for his country in Vietnam. His hands lay idle in his lap and his face was turned towards the window. His eyes were unseeing. His thoughts were going back in time, to a time when he grew up, apprenticed to his father to become a carpenter, going to church dances and movies or an ice cream parlour in the summer after work, sitting in the sun with his buddies and watching the girls go by.

He smiled to himself as he pictured the day when he saw Lizzy the first time and how, for some reason, his heart had started to beat faster when their eyes met. He had felt an uncommon heat rush through his whole body.

"Who is that?" he had asked his friends. They had laughed and told him she was living on the edge of town with her family and they were all kind of weird. "You wouldn't even get a kiss let alone touch her breast," big bully Bruce had said. Gary remembered how he actually had felt angry towards the guy. How would he know? He couldn't get her out of his mind. All he had thought about was how to see her again.

In a way I was 'forewarned' went through his head. He had started taking walks in the area where she lived. Once he saw her in her parent's garden. He stopped at the fence, greeted her and reminded her that they had seen each other at the ice cream parlour. He complimented her on the beautiful garden. The sunflowers were blooming and their huge heads were all turned towards the sun. He commented on it and she explained they do that, in the mornings they face east, at noon they face south, later

131

they would turn their heads west, always looking at the sun. He didn't know that and was genuinely surprised. It had pleased her to know something he didn't.

Gary took a deep breath. He had taken it slow, never stayed long, never asked her out, and in time she trusted him and he noticed she seemed to wait for him. She was always in the garden when he came along. Often he had taken his bike right after work to be faster and still be home for dinner. One day her dad had been in the garden as well. He had asked him in for a coffee. Lizzy's mother was a homely sort, and very quiet. He felt he was being appraised. The man wanted to know all about his family, his job and what his plans for the future were. As Gary left he placed a hand on his shoulder and told him he had no objection if he wanted to take his daughter out. "Oh my goodness", he thought now, "I think I turned awfully red in my face. All I could say was thank you, sir."

"My Lizzy", he whispered to himself, "soon, very soon now I can take you in my arms again. And I'll finally meet my little daughter". He took a photograph out of his breast pocket and looked at the two people who meant the world to him. He had married Lizzy two years after her parents had approved of him. Since his parent's house had an extra room next to his they were welcomed to start their married life there. He had been nearly twenty-two when he was drafted and Lizzy had been two months pregnant. He thanked God for his parents who had promised to look after his wife and baby while he was in the army, far away. He had worried but all Lizzy's letters were positive. When he received the news he was the father of a little girl he was the happiest man in the world. They had christened her Lori Ann. She had the fair blond looks of her mother but the dark eyes from his father. He had not been able to go on leave because he had been wounded and could not travel. The war was gruesome. He had to do things he would rather not think of let alone talk about.

It was a horrible day when he got the news both his parents had been killed in a freak accident. It still took a few months before they let him go home to look after his wife and daughter and sort out his parent's estate. It unsettled him that Lizzy had stopped writing but he also was in a rather remote area and the postman just did not call there. He was glad to be alive. Many of his comrades had been killed, often right next to him.

Finally the train rolled into the station and he got off with a pounding heart. His legs and his hands were shaking when he felt terra firma under his feet again. He looked at the people in ordinary clothing, hoping to see a familiar face. Everybody hurried off to their destination. He could have taken the bus but decided to enjoy the first walk through his old town. He smiled and greeted everyone, he felt alive again, knowing Lizzy and little Lori Ann were not far away. "I made it back", he said aloud, and the people passing him grinned and nodded. He was still wearing his uniform. A "Closed" sign was across the door of his father's workshop. One of his neighbours seemed shocked when he yelled "Hi, Bill". His right hand went up as if to say "Stop Gary" – but Gary was already around the corner heading for the house entrance. In this town nobody locked their doors, so Gary quietly opened the house door and called "Lizzy, I'm home!"

He stepped into the house, the rather large hall was bare of any furniture, the drawing room to the right was empty and so was the dining room to the left. He walked through to the kitchen and even here everything had a not-lived-in-look about it. The fridge doors were open, it was clean and no food of any kind was anywhere, not even in the pantry. With a sinking feeling he went upstairs to check the bedrooms. They seemed much larger because there was nothing but emptiness. A letter with his name

on it was taped to his old bedroom door. It was from Lizzy. He
was afraid to open it. He just knew it was bad news. She
reminded him that she had been very young when he left. He had
been away for a long time, life had gone on; she had met
someone else and had applied for a divorce. The papers were at
his parent's lawyer. She had sold all the furniture when she
needed money. Since his parents had left the house in his name
alone she had not been able to sell it.

Gary sank down against a wall sobbing hard. He couldn't
control it. He was sitting on the floor of a totally empty house, his
parent's dead, his wife and the child he had never met gone. He
had been fighting for two years in a war of which he did not
approve. It wasn't his war, and now his life was empty. Empty
like this house, empty like the fridge in the kitchen, empty of the
people he loved and it would have been better had he been killed
in Vietnam…

The worst shock was the lawyer's revelation that Lizzy had
teamed up with Bruce, the guy who had told him years ago you
wouldn't get a kiss from her, let alone touch her breast. Now
Bruce had not only his wife but also his daughter, the little girl he
was longing to see.

"I will fight for my daughter," he promised the lawyer, "I
will never give up."

36: It Was the Wrong Date...

Grace was close to tears all the time. She knew her beloved companion did not have many more days to live and she just couldn't imagine her life without him. She worked at the library, only ten minutes away from her home. At lunchtime she would run back to see how he was doing and trying to get some food into him. The last few weeks had been hard. He was now totally blind, eating very little, he was dizzy and unsteady and she had to put diapers on him and almost wished it would be over soon. She did not have the heart to bring him to the vet to have him put out of his misery.

"Oh, Helen," she breathed, "I love Pepper so much, how can I be the one to kill him? I just can't see myself making the decision."

Helen tried to make her feel a little better by telling her about her own memories about her and her father's pet.

"I understand. I lost a dog once, but it was different. Mandy was run over and I cried for six weeks until my seven year old boy insisted on getting another dog. It was never the same. I remember my father shooting his beloved cat Peter; whom he had had for twenty-one years. Dad cried after he did it. He explained to me he was being kind to Peter who was suffering and dying anyway. And, Grace, - you would be kind to Pepper. What kind of life is this for him? He suffers, Grace, and you don't have to shoot him. The vet will give him a needle and he will gently fall asleep."

It took a few more days before Grace did what had to be done.

It was about two months later. Helen ran into her in Perkys Coffee Bar. She looked fine to her, almost happy. Giving her a big hug she couldn't help asking:

"Heh, you, how are you doing? Did you get another dog? You seem happy to me!"

Pointing to the chair next to hers Grace offered Helen some newton fig cookies but said:

"Here, have some date squares, you want a coffee?"

Grace's face almost split with the biggest smile spreading from ear to ear:

"I am happy, Helen, I really am! You wouldn't believe what I did! I'm embarrassed to talk about it… and I don't want to 'jinx' it…"

"Oh, come on. We know each other long enough. What did you do? And, by the way, you are eating newton fig cookies and not date squares."

"Whatever. Okay, I'll spill my beans but promise to keep my secret for now. I couldn't stand living alone after Pepper was gone. One night I went online and checked out the dating sites. I figured it would be nice to have a human companion I could travel with instead of another dog who keeps me at home. You know, I lived with Pepper for ten years after my lousy divorce, convinced 'a dog is a woman's best friend' but I'm getting older and I want a bit more out of life now before it is too late. Believe it or not, I have about three dates a week! I found a dating site for seniors with men looking for the same thing I was looking for, companionship."

Wow! Helen was dumb-founded. She looked at her, she was incredulous, and by now Grace was very excited to tell her all about her dates.

"I always meet them at Serious Coffee in Beachsville, I want to be safe. They don't need to know where I live. So far I have met each of them only once. I liked a few of the guys but none has even asked me for a second date. But there is one - Helen, - I am going to see him again on Saturday. But I have another date this afternoon. I feel like a teenager again. It's cool, maybe you should try it!"

When Grace met Helen a couple of weeks later she couldn't wait to tell her more about it.

Grinning, she confided:

"Remember the afternoon date I told you about? I was waiting for the new guy and low and behold, all of a sudden the one I had a date with for Saturday stood in front of me. You can't imagine my embarrassment! I felt the blood rushing to my face. I wasn't sure what to say, but he just sat down, smiled and complimented me on my healthy coloring."

"My goodness, Grace, - what a situation! What did you do when the other guy turned up?"

"That's the doozy, Helen, he never did! It was this one I had the date with. During our coffee I told him about my mistake and we had a good laugh and the laugh settled it. We have been seeing each other quite a bit and are planing to go on a trip to the UK in August. So? What do you say now?"

It was almost a year later when Helen worked alongside Grace at a volunteer function. When there was a bit of a lull Grace held her left hand in front of Helen's face and looked at her expectantly.

"My goodness", Helen exclaimed, "you got married?"

"Helen, he is incredible. I had an accident resulting in a broken hip and he cared for me. I lived with him for several months, he really proved himself. When he asked me to marry him I agreed wholeheartedly. My home is for sale and I will live with him. When I sold my car, he immediately had his transferred into both our names. I was so very lucky to meet him and he thinks all the luck is on his side. We are so happy. Can you imagine what it's like to have a new start like this in our ripe old age?"

"Congratulations Grace! Do you remember the day when you introduced him to me? I had told him you were a keeper. He seems to have taken it to heart. Please tell him I am glad you two will be together for the rest of your life."

"Bet ya, Helen, I'll do whatever it takes to keep him and myself healthy. We look forward to many travels before we get too old. Once we cannot travel anymore we might get a dog."

Hope. There is always hope!

37: Hope You are Not Superstitious

The apartment was in a gorgeous building. It was the very first high rise built in West Vancouver with ten floors and forty six suites.

The Real Estate person had told me it had been a prize winning architectural design. It had a curved front and all the balconies were finished with tiles like cut up pipes. The jokers in town said they were "wine racks".

I loved the lobby. The floor to ceiling front glass wall was facing south; it was bright and airy and had a fountain in the center, a sofa and two comfortable chairs. During construction people came to stare at the growing height.

West Vancouver only had houses with one or two floors during those years. The builder tried to sell "condominiums". The concept was unknown: you buy a house but not an apartment! He only had a few takers. Because of it the original builder went bankrupt. He had used only the best materials and the second one finished the closets and kitchen cabinets with cheaper materials. Most of the beautifully laid out apartments were originally rented.

Every suite was facing the ocean. The views of Vancouver City across the Burrard Inlet, the Lions Gate Bridge, Stanley Park and on clear days Vancouver Island were spectacular. Sail boat regattas, fishing boats and cruise ships added to the picture. There were one bedroom suites, smaller two bedroom suites, larger two bedroom suites and only four very large three bedroom suites. One of the bedrooms of all the larger two and three bedroom suites was located on the north side overlooking the small houses built in rows halfway up the coastal mountains, wonderful to look at when their tops were covered with snow.

One day, waiting in front of the elevator door I heard people talking a floor below in the parking garage. The elevator door was being held open and made rattling noises as it tried to close itself. When it finally came up to the lobby I entered and said "Hi" to the friendly looking lady already on board.

"Hi, Miss", she smiled, "my name is Marge and I am the caretaker of this building. Are you visiting?"

"No. I bought Mr. Bailey's suite. I want to take some measurements before I move in."

"Oh! Congratulations! It's a nice place. I hope you are not superstitious. Well, I'll be seeing you."

With that she exited on the fourth floor. Apprehension built within me as I continued up to the eighth floor. I had just come from the lawyer who had handed me my keys. To the right was *MY DOOR*! While I was still trying to fit the right key into the lock the door beside me was opened rather abruptly. It made me jump. A tiny, pale white haired lady peaked around the corner and stared at me:

"Oh," she said, "I thought someone was breaking in. Are you the new owner?"

"Yes", I replied. She looked at me with her steel blue eyes and exclaimed:

"Congratulations! You bought a beautiful place. I just hope you are not superstitious." She was about to withdraw when I stopped her: "Wait a minute, why did you say that? You are not the first one to make that comment. What is this about?"

Coming a step closer she confided in a low voice: "Two women died in there, mother and daughter, first the mother, then a year later the daughter, in the master bedroom in the same bed, on the same day, at the same hour."

She explained the widower, a man of over ninety, had never used the room again and had slept in the back bedroom. A

140

grandniece was his only family now. For several years after moving into a care home he did not want to sell the apartment which held so many memories for him. His grandniece brought him to visit it occasionally. When he was ninety-four and not well she persuaded him to let it go.

So that was it! I had met the grandniece when she sold all the furnishings. Her aunt had been an artist. The walls had been covered with her work. All the paintings were sold except for one, a rather large one of oriental lilies in soft pink, green and lilac tones. I did not think it valuable enough to pay the price she was asking. I told her to leave it and then something of her aunt's beauty loving soul would remain.

With mixed feelings I entered the apartment. I walked up the long hallway towards the kitchen, stood a moment in front of the sink and enjoyed the view out of the west facing window. I turned and went into the living room. My heart soared! The room was bathed in sun light. It was large, very bright and absolutely gorgeous. The front wall was glass from floor to ceiling. To the left was an oversized sliding glass door to the large balcony. I stepped out and felt as if I was in a dream. The ocean shimmered and glistened, a light breeze curled the silvery water slapping against the rocks of the Seawall. Tug boats, sail boats, fishing vessels and the cries of many seagulls enchanted me. Vancouver Island was barely visible.

To the west a lighthouse at the end of the mountain range on a high rock jutting out to sea looked solid, trustworthy and eternal. It blinked at me. At least I thought so… I inhaled the salty sea air deeply and understood why the old gentleman could not let go of this place after he lost both the women he loved.

"No", I said aloud, "I am not superstitious." I thought it kind of him to let them die at home and not in the hospital. The daughter, sick already when the mother died, might have cried herself to death on the first anniversary of her mother's passing. I wandered into the front bedroom, the room in which they had both died. There were the lilies, the painting which did not sell. I looked at it, talked to it, promised to love this place just as they had done. The flowers seemed to grow towards me, reach out to me. Yes, I thought, I can handle this, it is all right. I'll respect their spirits.

It was fall. I had lived in the apartment for more than a year. One dark evening, I decided to bake a cake. Standing in front of the sink I was mixing the dough with a hand mixer when I heard the happy laughter of two women behind me in the hallway towards the entry door. A cold chill ran down my spine. I just knew I was not alone. I slowed the mixer and turned it off. Ever so carefully I turned around and willed myself to walk down the hall to check the door. The dead bolt was in place, the safety chain was on. Nobody could have come in. I opened the closet doors when it dawned on me: "It must be them." So I started talking to them, soothingly, and hearing my own voice helped me to calm down. I felt terribly alone, yet not alone. On unsteady feet I went back to the kitchen and continued mixing. After all the ingredients were added I filled the cake form and put it in the oven.

There! There it was again, this time close to my kitchen entrance. Now it was more like a giggle, a secretive chuckle and I heard quick running feet right behind me. I hunched my back and felt my hair stand up, I wanted to scream. Heavens, I was a grown woman.

"Come on, Giselle, be realistic! Your mind is playing tricks. You are overtired." Again, I willed myself not to lose control of my actions. Slowly I turned and tip-toed towards the living room where they had gone. I talked to them again before I switched the light on. There was nothing, absolutely nothing. But the room seemed grey, strangely quiet and empty. The painting with the lilies now in the living room appeared darker than usual. The clock on the book shelf showed nine thirty. My heart was racing. My skin had goose bumps, my scalp prickled.

An hour later the cake was done. I went to bed in the room in which they had died all those years ago. I had a water bed and I was happy it had a box under it tightly hugging the floor. Did you think I felt safer because nobody could hide under the bed? You betcha!

When I left my apartment to go to work in the morning, my neighbour with the steel blue eyes yanked open her door:

"Giselle, have you heard? Mr. Bailey died last night around nine thirty."

I felt faint. "Oh my God", I whispered more to myself than to Mrs. White. She stared at me: "Why are you so shocked? You didn't even know him!"

It seemed impossible but she turned even paler than she was when I told her about my experience the night before, exactly at the time he died. She whispered: "I told you. I warned you. But you thought you were not superstitious. You even told me you could handle it. You see? I always believed there is more between heaven and earth than meets the eye."

They never visited me again. I lived peacefully and happily in the apartment where they died for nearly twenty-five years.

The painting with the lilies has been with me ever since. I had tried to sell it when I moved to the Island, but it never sold. I am looking at it while writing this…

38: Oh my, an Affair with Omar Sharif ?

We were sitting in a small Pizza Restaurant on Stafford Street in Winnipeg, just around the corner from my skin care business. I don't remember the exact year. Miss L. from CBC Radio had asked me for lunch. Ms. L. had interviewed me already several times, we liked each other. Actually I admired her. She was quite smart and she was a good interviewer. At one point she confided "I know I am not pretty but I am good at what I do. They will never let me do TV interviews. If I had a choice to be either beautiful or intelligent – next time I would choose beautiful. Right now I have to deal with being intelligent." She was right and radio suited her. For me, it would have been a difficult question. I thought 'I am glad to have both…' without saying it. Vain? Hmm. Her next comment totally floored me:

"Giselle, tell me the truth. How, when and where did you meet Omar Sharif? Is it true you two met in Las Vegas?"

Omar Sharif? How would I know Omar Sharif? I didn't know Omar Sharif and I told her so. She did not give up.

"Come on Giselle, this affair of yours is a great news story, come on my program and let me interview you about it. And don't deny it, - it's all over Winnipeg. I had it confirmed by a reliable source."

"But L., it is not true! I only know him as an actor from the movie 'Dr. Zhivago' and from the bridge section in the Free Press. Why would a famous man like him be interested in me? Besides, he is a very heavy smoker and a well-known gambler at the Monte Carlo Casino often making a fortune and at other times losing it again. Everything I know about him would not in the least fit my lifestyle."

I was trying to make light of it by telling her how I had cried when he, in the film, collapsed and died of a heart attack on the sidewalk in Moscow. He had been in a streetcar when he saw Lara, got out and was running after her. She never turned around and he never caught up with her. It was so terribly sad. It was not a happy ending of the movie "Dr. Zhivago". I sat in the cinema and saw it with my eight month old son on my lap who had been so good during the long hours.

I could not convince L. She was sad and expressed how she had thought I had more trust in her and left, disappointed in me. I felt upset and said:

"L., I am telling you the truth. I would like to know who your 'reliable source' is." Naturally she would not reveal this information. Her parting words were:

"Why don't you phone him and then give me a call. Let me know if Sharif is okay with you telling the story."

A few days later I walked, as I regularly did, through my store greeting and exchanging a few words with my customers in every section; first at the manicure tables, then the facial and massage cabins and last the pedicure room. This was an open area with five special chairs side by side. All five chairs were occupied. We were very busy since I had taped a TV show showing a pedicure on a man. A well-known Winnipeg lawyer, one of our regular manicure customers, was my model. He pretended to be shocked when I tried to remove his socks. We were already "On Air":

"What? You have to take off my socks? If you had told me that earlier I would not have agreed to be your guinea pig."

He was joking but this show brought a lot of new customers into the pedicure section. One of the ladies getting her feet done tried to keep me close by asking all kind of questions relating to my business and my frequent travels for lectures and health

146

related conventions. I did not really know her, but I knew of her. She was a freelance journalist and very much into society gossip. I wasn't quite sure where she was going with her interrogation. Finally she asked me the question switching on the light in my head:

"You know what, Giselle? I would love to go to Monte Carlo with you. Let's make it a fun trip. Maybe we can meet Omar Sharif and you can introduce me to him. What do you say? I am serious!"

It was much the same as with L. from CBC. The woman laughed and did not believe me.

"Sure", she said, "I would not admit it either!"

The other four customers sat there looking at me with open mouths and curious eyes, none of them getting involved in the conversation. The five employees kept their eyes on their customer's toes. When I finally walked away I was thinking about the implications with now even more people spreading this ridiculous rumour. I was shaken by the second time a journalist brought it up. Me, - having an affair with Omar Sharif? How ridiculous. I decided it was time to check with my lawyer. He grinned and then asked me,

"Giselle, is this true? Did you meet him in Las Vegas at the last convention you attended? Why not admit it, why should he not be a good friend to you?" I was firm in denying all of it. Finally he advised me:

"You know what? Let them talk. The next time you are confronted with it just smile and say 'no comment' and let it be. I must say I get a kick out of it and, if nothing else, it's good for business."

He was right. We had more business, new people booked appointments hoping to catch a glimpse of me. For a short time I was a bit of a celebrity. When my second stepdaughter invited me to her upcoming wedding she added,

"But please, don't bring Omar Sharif."

I looked at her, surprised she brought up the gossip.

"You too? You don't believe it, do you? It's so ridiculous…"

Without looking up from the manicure she was doing, her answer was "Oh yes, I believe it."

"Would it be alright if I invited the ABBA Band?" I knew her fiancé loved this band.

"I would have to ask Dad about it. He's paying for the wedding." (We were separated)

She was serious while I was joking. One of my wedding gifts was the newest album of the ABBA group.

After a few weeks everything died down and nobody ever mentioned it again. I tried for weeks on end with little comments, statements or questions to find the 'reliable source' within my employees. To my surprise I succeeded a couple of years later. It was my expression "Oh my…" that I had uttered, "Oh my" when my secretary came and reminded me of a phone call she had put on hold ten minutes ago. "Oh my, oh my…" started it all. Weird, eh? Translate "Oh my oh my" into "Omar..." Since there was only one Omar known worldwide the rumour was born and quickly escalated. "Oh my, - Omar was waiting on the telephone to speak to Giselle..."

Moral of the story: Be aware of how clearly you pronounce your words!

This whole episode came back to me after I read the news of Omar Sharif's passing subsequent to a heart attack in Cairo on July 10th 2015.

RIP my good old friend!

39: My Friend, the Green Turtle

One should never snorkel alone – but what do you do if you don't have anybody to snorkel with? Give up? That is not in my make-up! So I did snorkel on my own. Usually I didn't swim too far from the beach but this time I swam straight out towards the horizon. I knew there was a reef across the bay and the sharks were on the other side of it. Looking beneath me I did not see a single colorful fish. I was always searching for the Humu Humu Nuku Nuku Apua'a, the Hawaiian State fish. I loved the colouring, the design as if a young child had painted it. Lots of corals and seaweed were under me here in the Anaeho'Omalu Bay on the Big Island and it looked rather dark. I just kept my face down, hoping to see something and kept on swimming.

You know how the sixth sense kicks in when someone watches you? I definitely had that sensation. I remembered when once in Cuba people were waving and screaming at me from the beach and when I looked around a barracuda, about two thirds of my body length was swimming next to me. The waters in Cuba are very clear and I was not too far from the beach. I kept my cool and did not make any hasty movements and after a few more metres the huge creature turned away. Naturally, the shock came later when all the people at the beach started talking to me at once. But now, on the Big Island of Hawaii, with all the darkness beneath me, it was different.

When I looked to the right I was so shocked I let go of my mouth piece and swallowed water. A small head on a long neck sticking out from a plated body was turned directly towards me, observing me with large slanted bulging eyes. It was a rather large "Green Turtle". The Hawaiians call it 'hona'. I was treading water and tried to get my breathing under control again while the

149

turtle waited next to me. It then started to swim a few strokes, waited, looked back at me as if to say "come on…" and when I tried to turn around it kind of coaxed me to keep swimming next to it. I knew they were not dangerous, so I did what it seemed to suggest. After maybe another fifty metres it veered to the left. There was a great big light spot in the sea, lit up by the sun. Coming closer I was surprised to see a huge circular pit with light sand probably about thirty metres wide and quite deep. With the seaweed earlier I had no idea how deep the ocean under me was, - and this, so totally unexpected, was an incredible sight. The sunlight was filtering down and the movement of the sea caused changing shapes and shadows just like an enormous kaleidoscope.

My turtle stopped a moment beside me as if enjoying my surprise, looked me in the eye and then swiftly descended for just a few seconds, came back up clearly inviting me to come down visiting with its family. I counted thirteen turtles, - five of them very large and the others all of different sizes, even some small ones. Growing children, I thought. They seemed to congregate in groups of three or four. I couldn't help staring down at all this beauty for a couple of minutes before I felt a shiver and realized I had to head back. But now I knew what my friend had been up to. It had a purpose for accompanying me; it wanted me to see this little wonder in the middle of the dark ocean. I watched it while it joined a group of three its own size and one smaller one. Another shiver went through me and I turned and started to swim back towards the beach.

I hoped to get a bit warmer using strong movements but I soon realized I was in trouble. I half expected my turtle friend to come back and help me on my return but it did not happen. A few times I was ready to give up. I was awfully cold and tired. Hypothermia, my brain registered. I knew my friend Elsa was at the beach waiting for me and was probably already worried. The beach was much farther away than I had realized swimming out. I had been too curious about what the turtle wanted from me to pay much attention. I had seen a small paradise. Would it cost me my life? Finally, the last few metres walking to the beach with my flippers in my hands were almost too much. I fell onto the sand, Elsa was there with a big towel, she covered me and I immediately went to sleep. Maybe I fainted. She and six other people stood around me when they woke me after two hours. I was lucky the sand and the sun had been warm.

It was an incredible experience but I warn you: Do not, under any circumstances, swim or snorkel too far from shore. Remember you need more strength for the return since your body temperature will have gone down. It just makes you so very tired and it would be too easy to just give up. This was not the first time I just made it.

A couple of years later I visited the Big Island again but stayed in another area with a much smaller bay. The snorkeling was wonderful with lots and lots of colorful fish. One didn't even have to swim more than maybe twenty metres. It was also easy to get in and out of the water as there was a sandy beach. One day, resting with my adopted brother under a tall palm tree I noticed there were absolutely no waves, just small ripples. I wondered why nobody was at the beach or in the water. The palm tree above us bent almost half way down indicating quite a strong wind. Since the water seemed so calm I told Heinz I'll check on my pretty fish, I won't stay long. Looking around, my face under water I couldn't see anything, not even the rocks I knew so well. I checked my snorkeling glasses but they were clear. I kept looking and still couldn't see anything. I lifted my face and was shocked to see myself almost in the middle of the ocean. At least, it seemed like that, I was far away from the shore. An underwater tow had pulled me way out in seconds. I almost cried. How would I ever be able to get back? It seemed impossible. I thought of my son and the will to see him again gave me the will to fight my way back. Now the waves were coming right towards me. If I wouldn't have been a kayaker I would not have known how to get over large waves, I started swimming about a hundred metres to the right taking the waves sideways, and then turning, I did the same to the left. I added many extra metres to my journey and when I reached the sides of the small bay surrounded with huge lava rocks with razor sharp edges I had trouble trying to keep myself away with the strong current pushing me towards them. I was exhausted. Without flippers I would never have made it. A few times I felt like giving up, just like I had felt in the Anaeho'Omalu Bay when swimming with the turtle. I encountered a small shark closer to the rocks. I was shocked but glad I had not even thought of that danger. Maybe they were also way out at sea.

Heinz was standing close to the edge of the water, gave me a hand and pulled me up to the sand. My knees buckled and I had to sit down, half in the water, half on the sand.

"I couldn't see your snorkel anymore and was almost ready to go for help but I didn't want to leave here. Am I ever glad you made it back."

When we walked towards the hotel about 200 meters away we saw all the red flags, the warning you shouldn't enter the ocean. The life guard hearing my story shook his head.

"I can't believe you made it back. We would have had trouble coming out with the life boat to get you. You were very, very lucky."

I have learned my lesson: Never snorkel alone and always check the colour of the flags indicating danger.

40: Candies and Cookies

She was impatient. She was trying to phone her sister in Hamburg but there was no answer. It wasn't night yet overseas, she had made sure of that. There was a nine hour time difference and it was only about 8.00 PM in Hamburg. Krystal wouldn't be in bed that early. Finally, after the seventh ring her sister picked up the phone.

"Hello! Hello! Is that Krystal? Yes? Thank goodness you are there. I need to talk to you."

"Oh, hello Gemma! Where is the fire? You haven't phoned for a while. Is everything alright? Why do you need to talk to me? I just came from the gym and was about to take a shower."

"Believe it or not, I am coming to Germany. I want to book my ticket. I'll be at the spa again and I was wondering if you could come as well. I'll arrive on the 10th of September and stay three weeks. Same place. It would mean so much to me to see you. I phoned Anna and they do have rooms for us. It's been a few years, Krystal. There are some serious things we have to talk about. It's better we do it in person."

"Serious things? What do you mean? Did you hear from Dad regarding the will you talked him into? Has he finally agreed to make one? You know I don't want to get involved. He can do what he wants. I guess you are right, he should have a will. But I don't care if he leaves me something or not, we can't make use of it anyway. I don't plan to go to East Germany anymore. It doesn't make sense to go there and exchange 25.00 West-Marks for 25.00 East-Marks for each day I'm there. I have to work hard for my money and can't afford to throw it away like that. You know one can't spend it there anyway. There is nothing worth buying. Mom gets upset and doesn't take it so I usually give it to Dad and he doesn't want it and just gets mad. He always wants to give me more. So, tell me, what's the use?"

"Krystal, Mom and Dad are getting on. Wouldn't you like to see them again before it's too late? If I didn't live across the ocean I surely would try to see them at least every two years. You are only a four or five hour train ride away. But that's not what I was going to ask you. I wanted to know if you would come with me if I come a week earlier, rent a car, pick you up and we surprise them? I think they would be very happy."

"Stop, Gemma, no - I don't want to go there. Besides, I have made other plans. As a matter of fact I'll leave just a couple of days after you finish your spa cure. Marie Ann is coming with me. I have traveled with her before and she is okay with me not wanting to share a room. I'd rather pay the single supplement and she agreed."

"Oh, Krystal, that is too bad. Where are you going this time?"

"Turkey. Very different from Thailand or Bali. The magazine from the travel agent listed some nice places and it's cheap, really cheap. We are looking forward to it. There is a nice sandy beach, lots of lounges and chairs on the lawn adjacent to it, trees for shade or you can get an umbrella. The big hotel has a very large swimming pool with a bridge across it, music every night, a restaurant and a bar. Breakfast and dinner is included. It is in a nicely landscaped, parklike setting with a high wrought iron fence around it. But we are staying in their small hotel outside of it, not quite one kilometer away. They have a shuttle bus in case it gets too dark to walk. Just outside the fence are several little Turkish shacks, some with souvenirs and others with bars, music and a bit of dancing. Marie Ann likes that, but as you know, I could do without it."

"Jeez, I'm almost getting jealous. What's the name of the hotel? Where do you fly to?"

"God, you are asking a lot of questions. I'm not sure right now. I'd have to look at my travel documents. Can't remember those Turkish names."

"O.k. Krystal, look it up. Don't hang up, I'll wait!"

"Why do you want to know? It might take me a few minutes."

"Doesn't matter. I'm curious. Can't imagine what Turkey would be like. You know we travel to Hawaii or Mexico but Turkey must be quite different."

Gemma heard Krystal rummage around in some papers. She came back and just said:

"Antalya. We fly to Antalya and then take a bus to the hotel. It's about an hour away from the airport. The hotel name is "Arkadaslar ". We arrive there about 10.30 in the morning."

"Thanks, sis. Have a good time. Too bad you don't want to go and see our parents. I understand. But you need to know about the will and what Dad came up with. He had a talk with a lawyer and wanted to list us three sisters with equal parts. He found out we could only use 10.00 marks per day of the inheritance if we come to visit the DDR. Despite that we still have to exchange the 25.00 West-Mark per day. I finally talked him out of us three being equal. We are both in the west and can't make much use of it. I suggested he should leave it all to Emily since she is there and would surely look after them when they need help. He insisted it is not fair and he is so sure that times will change.

One sentence he repeated was "You'll see, sooner or later Germany will be united again. And then we'll also get compensation for Stresow. It can't stay like this, no way. And both of you will be glad to have some money here." I told him there's no way in hell that Germany will be re-united. The

Russians will never allow it. Anyway, I got a letter from the lawyer and by signing it I forego my lawful inheritance. You'll get the same and if you agree you'll have to sign it as well. You see, it would have been good to discuss this in person."

"Gemma, you know what I think. I'll sign it. There isn't much to inherit anyway. I know Dad saves every penny and Mom hardly has a chance to spend it. And they will never get compensation for what they lost in Pomerania. And if Emily looks after them she deserves it. It's all okay with me."

"Krystal, think about it. If Dad is right about a collapse of the DDR someday then they would get something. I have a list of everything they owned before we were evicted. It does amount to quite a bit. I don't need it, I have my business but for you it could make a difference in your old age."

"Come on, stop it. That will never happen. I'll sign it and forget it. You better stop talking. This call costs you a mint. Enjoy your spa cure. Maybe I will join you next time. Good night, Gemma."

Since Krystal did not want to come, Gemma gave up the plan to visit their parents in East Germany. Good thing she hadn't asked them yet to get a visitor visa and thereby get their hopes up. She went to Bavaria to the spa, enjoyed the pampering, the daily concerts and the wonderful walks and hikes and bike tours through the forest and across the green meadows. The weather was great. Life was good and a wonderful change without the daily stress at the business.

Once in Germany, Gemma booked a trip to Turkey for the day before Krystal would arrive. She was waiting in the lobby of the hotel 'Arkadasla' where she was staying. It was a large bus and a lot of people stood waiting to check in. Everyone received a glass of orange juice with champagne and the mood was joyous. Gemma mingled in order not to be seen right away.

Finally Krystal and her friend Marie Ann came in the door and joined the line-up for the reception desk. Gemma watched them and after they were registered they waited for their luggage, nursing their drink. With a casual flair Gemma walked towards them, looking at Krystal but pretending not to know her. Oh, Krystal's face! Gemma walked by and felt more than saw Krystal turning, looking after her. She turned around and then couldn't help it, a big smile split her face because Krystal's mouth was wide open and her eyes registered shock and disbelief. It just took a moment and they had their arms around each other. It was the first hug in their life – as it was something not done in their family.

"Oh my God, Gemma, I thought I was seeing a ghost. And then I thought you had a double. Now I know why you wanted to know where I was going! Wow!" She had tears in her eyes. Krystal had always been the tough one but she wasn't now.

The next day they were at the beach and in the water. There were no life guards but signs warning about rip tides. Disappointed because the water was not clear they headed towards the lawn, found three loungers side by side under an umbrella and settled down to get a sun tan. Gemma fell asleep. When she woke up Krystal and Marie Ann teased her, laughed and told her she had missed a lot of excitement. Small planes had been flying low back and forth over the beach dropping candies and other things over the adults on the lawn. All the kids had been running and screaming and the adults who didn't have children had joined in picking up what they could and they had done the same.

"We saved something for you, Gemma. Here, this is for you."

Gemma couldn't believe she had slept through all the excitement but took what was handed to her.

"Thank you, girls, that was nice of you. I don't eat candy but I love cookies."

She looked at the cookies. They were so light and very thin with a rim around them, wrapped in something like wax paper and Turkish writing was all around the rim.

"I have never seen cookies like this. It doesn't even feel as if there is something to them. The center is so thin."

Krystal and Marie Ann laughed until tears started running down their cheeks. Gemma thought they must have been drinking something...other than Turkish coffee. Maybe Turkish coffee with something else in it?

"Are you tipsy or what? Did you have Turkish coffee? Did you eat your cookies already?"

More laughter. Finally:

"Gemma, Gemma, you lady of the world. Do you really not know what those cookies are?"

A little annoyed about the two teasing her Gemma looked at them and threw the cookies back at them.

"Here! Eat them yourself."

She had never seen condoms before in her life.

41: Dog Days or Other Miserable Days

Dog Days were popularly believed to be an evil time when "the Sea boiled, the Wine turned sour, Dogs grew mad, and all other creatures became languid; causing to man, among other diseases, burning fevers, hysterics, and phrensies," according to Brady's *Clavis Calendaria,* 1813. End of quote.

Are those the days when I am not sure what is ailing me? I am sad, weak, down, tired, can't get going and somehow it seems the whole world is ganging up on me. If someone says something nice I feel they just want to put honey around my mouth. A stubborn donkey is growing and bucking up within myself and wants to kick the kind person... If someone says "come on, cheer up..." or even worse, "you have no reason to feel that way" I know they don't know what they are talking about. Can't I just feel bad without a reasonable reason? Can't you just let me be miserable? Leave me alone. Maybe that's what I need, 'lone-time' to find my centre again, to balance my emotions. Maybe I am stressed and I have gone too fast 'for my soul to catch up with me'. Time to slow down.

Have you ever thought about how tough it is to always pretend everything is alright? We keep smiling, we do what we have to do or think we have to do, give polite answers or the expected answers. In reality we would like to scream or throw even our best china against the wall. Before my back gave me trouble I would grab the vacuum cleaner and give it a real good workout. A couple of years ago I would spend hours in the garden, listen to the silence and let myself suffer through sometimes agonizing back pain without being able to stop before the job I had started was done. Mind over matter? What matter? The physical pain or the pain you can't put a finger on? The pain

159

accumulated during a lifetime without ever having had a chance to clear the air? Because there are things you just don't talk about. You don't want to trouble others with your troubles because they have their own troubles.

Okay. The most well-meaning people tell you to have counselling. I tried it. Pay for the pair of ears that will attentively listen to you. Sometimes you get asked intelligent questions but mostly they wallow in your misery, stir it up like pea soup, push it around and explain it from this side and the other and, by acknowledging it, they multiply it. In the end you start to believe life has dealt you some awfully bad cards. In your heart of hearts you know it's not quite true, that that wasn't the problem in the first place. Run while you can! But if you keep going back and enjoy listening to these smart people, after all, you want your money's worth, - in the end you start believing it. You like the new truth? It makes you feel 'poor me' but it feels good? You don't realize by dwelling on it you felt worse, but the worst is that you start seeing it as the 'true truth'. Some truth! Brain-washing! And by believing and talking about your (new) truth you unwittingly hurt the people who love you most and you push them away.

No, counselling wasn't for me. And psycho pills were not either. Why would the first one make me feel so sick that I had to throw up? Oh no, - I never took another. There was no way I would let anyone, or anything, alter my brain waves. I told myself to take the bull by the horns, face my demons and acknowledge them. Take stock. What was it that made me feel so miserable? Why the loss of energy and getting tired of not being able to defend myself against - other people's truth? Lies? Things? Circumstances? Fight against windmills? Take charge of your life, I told myself. And read 'smart' books like "The Road less traveled" and "I'm okay, you're okay."

You know what I just did? I broke a lot of china. I was venting. I talked about all the things that don't work, did not work for me. I remember part of a joke: A zebra came to God and asked if it was black with white stripes or white with black stripes. God looked at it and said

"That depends entirely on how you see yourself."

Let's get back to the very beginning of this outburst. So how do I see myself? Some days are better than others and things seem clearer. But as there is dark and light, bright and dull, up and down, dry and wet, day and night, good and bad, happiness and sadness, so your outlook changes. My way was to keep busy. Did I ever realize I might have exhausted my store of energy? No. I felt responsible to "keep going" like the rabbit on the battery. I forgot one important thing: Work and play, activity and rest, laughing and crying. There was nothing to laugh about? Too many of those "dog days"?

The antidote: Get a dog. It ties you down? You have to walk it, get up earlier or lose your freedom? You don't even realize what you would gain: unconditional love and lots of it, an incredible understanding of your troubles. It looks at you and transmits feelings without words. By owning and being responsible for a dog you may even extend your life.

Second best? Go visit a friend who has dogs. These creatures just know how to lift your mood, get your mind off anything that may ail you. They love you, they want you and they play with you and before you know it they have delivered the medicine you didn't even know existed:

"Doggie Medicine".

42: A Russian Rape Baby

Once upon a time I belonged to a group of older German women who loved to read poetry. We met once a month and each one of us picked a poem to read to the group. I loved Eugen Roth, a German poet who started each of his poems with "Ein Mensch…" (a human being) and he had written hundreds of them. Kurt, the husband of one of our ladies claimed he had read and knows all of them. I have written poetry, not enough to have a book printed but I had fun with it. One day I read a poem starting with "Ein Mensch…" and it was a rather lengthy one. Kurt exclaimed "I have never read that one. How is it possible? I know all of his poems."
He wondered where I had unearthed it and if it was in a book he did not know. When the chairperson noted that I had written it he did not want to believe it. Kurt is gone to the pearly gates, but the poetry club still exists, even now, twenty years after we started it.

I had moved away and only remained in contact with Elsa. A few years ago she had told me Stephan, the husband of another member had died and his wife Louise had moved into an apartment building in North Vancouver. She had been a very soft spoken lady and a bit shy. There was a fire in her building. She had knocked on many doors and in the end was overcome by smoke. The members of the group I had known got smaller also because of other calamities, e.g. Alzheimer disease, a suicide and people moving into care homes and giving up their cars. It is twelve years since I last had contact with the chairperson.

My phone rang a few weeks ago on a Saturday evening and, picking it up, I couldn't believe the voice. It was the chairperson I thought had also died after I had heard of several accidents with lots of broken bones. She told me that she just finished reading

163

my memoir and felt compelled to talk to me. She expressed her surprise that I had ever had the courage to 'open up and tell all.' Within the conversation I asked about the 'club' and now it was my turn to be surprised. It was going stronger than ever.

"Imagine", she said, "we are over twenty members now, mostly new ones. Something incredible has happened. I just need to tell you this after reading about the Russian rapes in your book. Remember Amelia? Yes? Her daughter is also in our group. Well, you won't believe it. At the November meeting Amelia apologized she would not read a poem but, instead, will tell us a story she has kept a secret all her life. She told us about her experiences during the Russian invasion of Silesia and the raping that went on. She was raped a number of times and had a child, a baby girl. The girl grew up thinking her Canadian husband was her father. Amelia said she would still not have the heart to tell her now if it wouldn't be in this, our private circle. No, her daughter does not know she has a Russian father. The daughter sat there, shocked, staring at her mother and asked 'Was it me?' but since she had no other siblings she slowly realized what a bomb shell had just exploded."

I was incredulous. I knew firsthand about all the rapes, had watched my own mother being raped and had an aunt who was pregnant because of having been raped. But to imagine sitting in a poetry group when you are going on seventy and learning in public of your parenthood? That the father you had loved was not your father at all but a beast who had forced himself on your mother? One of several rapists? I was glad to hear mother and daughter had a good cry and a tight hug, surrounded and supported by good friends. The daughter contacted the media and both were interviewed. They are still both part of the poetry group. Both women have forgiven the Russian who fathered the baby because both of them are happy to have had each other over

164

all those many years. The daughter is glad to know her mother does not have to carry this secret within her anymore.

Life surely has its surprises.

43: My Earthquake Experiences...

Earthquakes always happen far away. Living in the Prairies, there was no reason to think about them too much, just feeling terribly sorry for the people who suffered through one or even lost their lives. I was impressed by a movie about the 1906 San Francisco quake and I prayed that I would never, ever experience one. Once after a quake I drove along a highway in California. It must have been in the early eighties. I saw a "detour" sign but ignored it. After a few hundred feet a construction tape across the road appeared, and a big sign announced "Road Closed". A few cars were parked on one side. I parked as well and walked towards the small group of people about fifty feet ahead. I felt my heart fall to my feet and my stomach lurch up to my throat. The highway was gone as if it had been cut off by a giant hand and a deep long empty river was there in its stead, the highway all broken up at the bottom. The earth had opened up and swallowed the highway. I realized I might be standing on a very fragile piece of road, it might cave in any minute and I quickly turned around, rushed to the car and drove away, following the detour signs I should have followed in the first place. What do they say? "Curiosity kills the cat…"

In 1984 I moved to Vancouver, British Columbia. I found a beautiful apartment on the 21st floor on Beach Avenue, overlooking English Bay and Stanley Park. It was as close to Paradise as I could have come. One morning something woke me up. It was 7.30 and there was no need to get up. No tennis today. I was stretching and noticed the lamp over my bed, a bare bulb on an electrical cord, swinging slowly from side to side. I stared at it, thought I had one of my occasional dizzy spells. Was it the building because it was so high? The idea it could be a quake did not even enter my head. Later I read about it in the Newspaper.

It was the first time I felt the earth moving, no pun intended. It literally moved, or at least the building I lived in did. The second time was a few years later living in West Vancouver in a ten storey apartment building on the 8th floor. Because of its curved design, the "Crescent" was known to be the most quake safe building in West Vancouver. To add to it, West Vancouver is built on rock. I felt pretty good about my choice of home. One beautiful, sunny day when leaving my suite I fell against the hallway wall. Why did I still have to contend with those annoying dizzy spells? My feet were not quite finding the floor when I walked to the elevator, but I assure you, I wasn't drunk! Again, the next day the front page news was the report of an earthquake. The reporter talked about the importance of having an "Earthquake Kit" and keeping a pair of heavy shoes under the bed in case of glass from broken windows. He stressed the danger of gas leaks and other problems, such as twisted metal after the "BIG ONE" would hit. For several days everybody talked about going out and buying a kit. I wanted to do so as well. At first they were sold out and later I never got around to it. Everything went back to normal and the experience slipped into the back of everybody's mind. Life and daily chores took over again.

In 2005 I moved to Nanoose Bay on Vancouver Island. Our house was about 30 feet above the golf course below. I thought if we ever had a quake with a tsunami the water would rush through the golf course and we would not drown in it. Great! It also would be much easier to get out of the house, much better than being in a high-rise. It was recommended to stand in a doorway or crawl under a table. A booklet about earthquake preparedness and HELP signs were distributed at a community meeting. A couple of years came and went and we never talked or thought about the possibility of a quake again. Then, one morning I almost fell out of bed. I have the tendency to sleep close to the edge, so it was easy. But my head board was shaking! I realized this is the third time I received a warning from "Mother Earth".

Health reasons caused us to sell our house and in 2014 we moved into an apartment in town to be closer to conveniences like busses, shops, hospital and other services. Our entrance is next to the emergency stair exit on the fourth floor. So many years later the "BIG ONE" has still not struck. Last night, leaning into a corner of my big fat leather couch, feet up on a stool and enjoying a movie on television, I experienced quite unusual heart problems. I asked my partner to keep an eye on me because I felt weird. My heart was kind of jumpy. I had a sudden headache and pressed my hands against both sides of my head. I told him there might be a chance he might have to get me to the hospital. He looked at me and suggested we go to the hospital right now. "Yes", I said, "and then sitting in emergency the whole night. No, let's wait, I'll take my emergency heart drops, maybe it will get better."

This happened at 7.30 P.M. At 8.09 my 'normal' couch started to massage my back, like one of the "Relax" chairs in airports, it got stronger and stronger, the couch was shaking, I saw the plant on top of the high bookcase moving and the reading lamp was wiggling back and forth.

I called out "Trevor, we have an earthquake!"

He looked at me with a funny expression and asked "what are you talking about?" He was kneeling on the floor in front of the bookcase, putting together our new patio chairs. I pointed up "look at the plant, look at the lamp, look at the chandelier, everything is moving! My couch is shaking like crazy!" Now he believed it. I cried "Put it on Twitter! Maybe we are the first to notice it!" He did. It was 8.10 PM. I felt a few softer aftershocks or, should I say a gentler massage on my back. Trevor checked CBC's Twitter Page, - and there it was:

"BC's whole coast line experienced an earthquake. The epicenter is 96 km south of Port Hardy in the ocean. There is no danger of a tsunami. The shock has been felt all along the coast of Vancouver Island and Vancouver. It measured 6.7 on the Richter scale."

6.7! Wow, that is big, frightening really. Did we make a mistake moving into this West Coast style fourth storey timber apartment building, not at all like the concrete construction of the Crescent in West Vancouver?

"We have to get some big screws and screw the book cases to the wall, they could easily have fallen over and killed me", Trevor mumbled. I agreed. I decided to buy and always keep some trail mix and bottled water at home. But mostly it was important to find out what to do or where to go when the BIG ONE hits. I would not want to stay on this 4th floor. I am glad the concrete exit stairs are next to our door. Maybe we would be safer in the stairwell. When inquiring at the Strata Council it turned out the stairway was the recommended place. Incredibly the apartments on the lower floors did not feel the quake at all, just the 4th top floor and some people on the third floor reported a bit of shaking.

We still haven't been able to find any screws suitable to screw the high book case to the wall. Again, by now 'life' has taken over and nobody talks about the danger. But we are reminded by some smaller 'shakes' along our coastline again and again. The predicted "Big One" is definitely coming; we just don't know 'when'.

It can happen tomorrow, or it can happen in fifty years.

44: Vancouver Island Living

My long-time friend Amalu from Germany asked me during a phone call if, after our latest move, we were still living on Vancouver Island. "Why did you ever leave Vancouver and move to a small island instead of remaining in the world famous city of Vancouver?"

"A small island?" I laughed, "No way, it is not a small island. It is as big as all of England or even bigger. But not as many people live here. And the ones who do are the friendliest sort. It's up to you to make as many friends as you want. Neighbours look out for each other; there is less criminality, less traffic, fresh water and clean air."

My friend couldn't believe it. We talked about it for a while and I told her about the snow cupped mountains and the sea, the lakes and rivers, the majestic coast line, the two larger cities Victoria and Nanaimo where most people were living. I mentioned the Island Highway from Victoria to Port Hardy in the north. I told her about the wonderful beaches, the smaller islands, the native Indians. I told her about a kayak tour through the "Broken Islands", more than a thousand of them, how we fished with a line from our kayak and how an eagle stole our first fish, how we feasted on fresh oysters, picked up in clear waters with our paddles. I told her about the multi-colored sea stars, glued to the walls of a rocky island coast, the dolphins and the whales. I explained that there were several hot springs where everybody can jump in since nobody has ever thought of developing them into health centres and charging for their use as healing waters. That aspect was known and appreciated only by the native Indians.

She was blown away when I told her of Long Beach, the resorts along the west coast, the Wickaninnish Inn in Tofino and the others in mid island; of the incredible weekend we had in Sooke sitting in our own Jacuzzi bathtub, drinking a glass of champagne and eating chocolate dipped strawberries while listening to and watching the crashing waves of the Pacific Ocean outside our window.

"But" she asked, "don't you miss the cultural life, theatre, concerts, people? What about schools, colleges, universities? And shopping?"

"Oh, we have all that right here. Victoria offers lots of cultural life and Nanaimo has theatre productions and concerts. We might not have the international names of the stage but we don't miss them. We like our little theatre in Chemainus, one of the most photogenic villages in our neighbourhood, about an hour's drive from Nanaimo. Artists from all over the world came years ago and painted historic murals on all the buildings with empty walls. How we love the delightful little cafés and eating places, tucked away in hidden gardens, galleries and craft shops along the one village street, places with European or English imports appealing to the immigrants or tourists. If we feel like "big city life" we spend a weekend in Victoria, still on the Island, the most English city outside of the UK. Victoria, the capital city and the seat of government of British Columbia is only about 150 kilometers away, a wonderful drive over the mountains with beautiful vistas."

She still wasn't convinced the Island was just the right place to enjoy life, especially in retirement: "Don't you get island fever? What about travel, trains, airports?"

"No problem, Victoria and Nanaimo have Airports with good connections to International flights, Comox has one and other, smaller places have private companies with smaller planes.

There are busses but most people have several cars in the family. If we want to get off the island to spend a day in a city with millions of people going to and fro we take a ferry to Vancouver. One could take the car along but it is a nightmare to drive in Vancouver, there are too many vehicles, it takes ages to go somewhere and you have trouble finding a parking space. There are too many people on the sidewalks as well, everybody is hurrying to get somewhere; nobody smiles or looks at you. Some don't even see you as they are talking or busy texting and run you over if you don't get out of their way. You taste the gasoline exhaust in your mouth and one can hardly wait to get back onto the ferry and come home."

Home is on this wonderful island. Naturally my friend Amalu wants to visit and see it for herself. Can't say I blame her… She might never want to leave.

45: Change of Seasons...

What is it that affects people differently during those times determined by the calendar and the weather? Nothing touches my emotions more regarding the change from summer to fall than a poem by the German poet Rainer Maria Rilke, titled "Herbsttag" - "Autumn Day". I see myself wandering the lanes, looking down and pushing millions of colourful leaves with my feet, yellow-orange-red and even a bit of green left over. I am thinking of my long gone childhood days and the time when my children were digging themselves into piles of raked up leaves. My mood turns sentimental, even sad. Life seems so short looking back. There was the happy worry free time I shared with my great grandmother, trying to bite into an artificial apple when I had no front teeth, my beloved grandparents and the years when I was loved, protected and guided by my parents. I see myself with my aunts, uncles, cousins and friends. Four generations...and I remember many wonderful people I met throughout the years. In retrospect it seems I only did have very little time with any of them. How fast the generations have gone and how few of my loved ones, closer to my own age, are left. I am next in line, just a leaf blowing in the wind. I think of the many things I have done; the many things I wish I had done and the many things I might never be able to do now.

The poet Rainer Maria Rilke expresses these sentiments beautifully in his German poem which I have translated:

'Lord, the time has come
A beautiful summer is gone.
Your shadow on the sundials changed,
you let the winds blow over the fields.

Help the last fruit to ripen,
give them a few more, warmer days,
let them fulfill their destiny
and put the sweetness in the heavy wine.
Who has no house - will not build now.
Who is alone now will remain so, long.
Will lie awake, will read and write long letters,
will restless wander up and down the lanes, -
when the leaves are drifting...'

I can't make Rilke's poem my own. No translation does it
justice. Other than in his words one cannot express all he himself
felt when writing it. I sense him near me when I read it. I see
myself sitting in a comfortable chair in a corner of a cozy room,
watching him write, a green shaded lamp on his desk in front of
the window, bent over and his paper the only bright spot in the
surrounding shadows. I feel he wrote it for me. When I came
across it for the first time I choked, I knew I was receiving a
message. The poem evokes many feelings, feelings about the
past, feelings about giving thanks for the bounty of a season past
and feelings of loneliness, of impending doom, of death and still,
- feelings of hope invade my thoughts. Hope for another autumn
day when the sunlight brightens the colour of the leaves, makes
the reds deeper, the yellows brighter and turns the already dying
ones to copper. I shall push the leaves under my feet until they fly
up into the air, I shall act like a child again, I shall laugh with
joy... but am too embarrassed knowing there are people watching
me. I look at the remaining colourful leaves on the trees and
marvel about nature. An endless cycle of birth, death and rebirth,
and every season has its own colours. As every generation has
and still, all are blending into and are part of our life.
    'Lord, the time has come...'

The time has come to sort out your harvest, to put the garden to sleep after planting next year's crop, to reset the thermostat for more warmth and take the winter jackets out of storage. The time has come to be closer together with your loved ones, invite the lonely, share a warm drink and listen to each other's memories, the stories of the ever changing seasons of life.

Rainer Maria Rilke's 'Herbsttag' is a favourite of many German poetry lovers:

"Herr, es ist Zeit.
   Der Sommer war sehr groß.
Leg deinen Schatten auf die Sonnenuhren,
und auf den Fluren lass' die Winde los.

   Befiel den letzten Früchten voll zu sein;
gib ihnen noch zwei südlichere Tage,
dräng' sie zur Vollendung hin und jage
die letzte Süße in den schweren Wein.

   Wer jetzt kein Haus hat baut sich keines mehr.
Wer jetzt allein ist, wird es lange bleiben,
wird wachen, lesen, lange Briefe schreiben
und wird in den Alleen hin und her
   unruhig wandern, wenn die Blätter treiben.

46: I live here – what's your excuse?

Once upon a time I lived in a green flower filled city
alongside the sometimes peaceful, sometimes wild, Pacific
Ocean, deep blue with crowned white crested waves. I was living
as if in a dream, drinking in this beauty and wishing I had the
talent to paint it. I was devastated when my husband told me
about an exciting opportunity for him to move to a city in the
Canadian Prairie. He talked about Winnipeg. The city was known
as the Canadian Siberia with nine months of winter and the
coldest, windiest corner in the whole wide world at Portage and
Main, and only three months of hot summers with lots of
mosquitos. But, - Winnipeg was also known for its "dry" cold
and always blue sunny skies. Supposedly this climate is much
healthier than the "wet" rainy coast and the propensity for getting
rheumatism and arthritis. You can dress for the "dry" cold but the
"wet" cold gets right under your skin.

Another perk was that Winnipeg has no crime and is a good
place to bring up a family within beautiful residential areas.
Large lakes for summer fun were only about ninety miles away.
This Prairie city of about 270.000 in 1964 offered lots of cultural
and social life, clubs, theatre, concerts and the world renowned
Winnipeg Ballet, on a par with the Bolshoi Ballet Moscow and
the French Ballet troupes. One-hundred-and-four different ethnic
groups were living peacefully together with lots of their typical
eating places, visited and enjoyed by all. Eat in a different part of
the world every day! Winnipeg was well known for its friendly
people. Every vehicle licence plate advertises: "Friendly
Manitoba", the Canadian province where Winnipeg is located.

Life has a way of interrupting your life by channelling it into
a different direction. I lived in Winnipeg for twenty years,

became a corporate citizen, an employer, a Community TV producer before the winds of change blew me back to my green country at the Pacific Ocean. No, I can not paint paintings but I can paint pictures with words. So I became a writer. I wrote regularly for several American and Canadian magazines, completed two Health Guides and finally was convinced to write my memoir. I did and that book brought me back to Winnipeg recently for a week long promotion, a book launch and book signings in three big book stores. Winnipeggers still read and love the real thing: Books, physical books. Many mentioned they don't like eBooks. My book reading at a Rotary Club was well received and a CJOB radio interview reminded the listeners about my history within their fair city and many old friends, former customers and even former employees came to see me and say 'Hello'. The Shaw TV's Community Channel taped an hour long interview about the book and another program about my history in Winnipeg when my first name had been a household word. But Winnipeg is not the city I remembered. Its population has grown to nearly a million; they have a crime rate now but many more beautiful residential areas.

Let me tell you what startled me most after arrival and the drive from the airport to the midtown hotel: Winnipeggers were driving only grey cars. All the busses were grey as well. One cornflower blue VW Beetle stood out as the only colour spot as far as I could see down Portage Avenue - trying to avoid one pothole after another. You could not read any licence plates as they were covered with a thick grey coating. It dawned on me nobody washed their car during the winter to avoid having their door locks frozen. Right, I remembered! It was thirty-four years since I was living here. I learned the winters are not Siberian anymore and climate change is taking its toll. It was mid-March and the previous week they still had 24 below Celsius but now

180

for double digit degrees up to 18 above Celsius. The snow was gone but the sand, used to sprinkle over the ice was colouring everything: Cars and buildings and roads and if you didn't wear glasses, it got into your eyes, it covered your hair and it was impossible to keep your shoes clean longer than from the house door to your car.

My grandson Jack, born and raised in Winterpeg as the Winnipeggers lovingly call their city, told me:

"Omi, at the entrance to Winnipeg from the west there used to be a sign:

"Welcome to Winnipeg. I live here – what's your excuse?"

47: "Too bad it's Canada"

One of the most beautiful cities in the world is Vancouver in
British Columbia, Canada. It offers everything: Mild winters but
high enough mountains for the ski aficionado and situated only
about 120 kilometers from the town of Whistler, the world
renowned ski resort. If you like water sports you can hardly ask
for a more beautiful setting than Vancouver at the blue Pacific
Ocean for any type of boating, sailing, paddling, windsurfing,
motor boating, fishing and even swimming for many months of
the year. You like ships or bigger boats better? Vancouver has
one of the most gorgeous inner harbours and it hosts many cruise
ships during the summer months since it is the gateway to the
Inside Passage to Alaska. I can hardly imagine what Captain
Cook or Captain Vancouver must have thought or felt when they
happened upon this hidden gem in the late 18th century. All along
the coastline were old growth forests, wildlife was plentiful and it
surely didn't take long for settlements to appear after it was
discovered.

Fishing and saw mills and later the arrival of the railway
brought hundreds of new settlers. Many warehouses were built.
The story of "Gassy Jack" is interesting, (use your imagination
why "gassy") a Yorkshire man who noticed there was no saloon
available for the many men. He was smart enough to offer to start
one. With eager help from all the thirsty men it was built and
finished within a few days (some say overnight) and soon women
appeared to add to the fun. The area, originally known as
Granville was later renamed after "Gassy Jack" and became
"Gastown". Nowhere could you find more drinking
establishments than right here. Over the years and as the city of
Vancouver grew this area went into decline and the warehouses

were falling into disrepair. Squatters, hippies and many artists had taken over. The area with its architecturally interesting old buildings was rescued in the 1970s when Gastown was declared the most historic part of Vancouver. Tourists now flock to Gastown because of its quaint artsy flavour. It became one of the prettiest and surely most interesting parts of Vancouver. It has many wonderful and diverse restaurants and "Gassy Jack's" statue is a popular photo stop. Not even a mile down the road is Chinatown, another touristy area of Vancouver.

An unforgettable sight is the castoff of cruise ships in the cruise ship harbour and sailing towards the Lions Gate Bridge, along the rich and very beautiful coastline of West Vancouver, the most expensive real estate and retirement place in Canada. You sail through a dreamland as the ship finds its way through the Salish Sea (formerly Strait of Georgia) with majestic snow cupped mountains turning red with the sunset. Unbelievably lovely views greet you while passing Haida Gwaii, a collection of islands at the most westerly point on the North Coast of British Columbia. Most people are more familiar with the name "Queen Charlotte Islands" as these islands were originally named. Prince William and Kate Middleton named their baby girl after Queen Charlotte.

I was asked once if I knew how God created certain areas on Planet Earth.

"Tell me", I replied and this is how it was explained: The different tribes had to line up and when it was their turn they were asked to give their reasons for what kind of land and how much they wanted. Most of them got what they asked for within reason. The Bavarians were very shy and stayed behind until there was hardly any land left when God noticed them. "You get a pretty region" God told them, "because you are not pushy and you waited. I kept the best for last" and therefore Bavaria and adjoining Switzerland is so beautiful and many people travel there just to see the landscapes and experience the joyful and friendly people who live there. If you ask me, I must say the British Columbia coastline and a sailing experience from Vancouver to Alaska is an incredible feast for the eyes. God must have had more surprises to hand out because this area is wider, grander and totally unforgettable. Yes, somewhat different because of the Pacific Ocean and it has nothing of the dollhouse prettiness you find in Bavaria or Switzerland.

Once, coming back from one of my many cruises to Alaska, I was sitting at a large table indoors with a group of eight or ten Americans enjoying a hot drink. Everybody had admired the glaciers and the calving with large sections of ice breaking off and crashing into the sea. They talked about the mighty ice rivers and the ice floats with seals or seabirds on them and as we were sailing on the still waters along the shores of Haida Gwaii one of the gentlemen, dreamily watching the ever increasing loveliness of the surroundings, expressed his feelings:

"I can't believe how beautiful all this is. Too bad it's Canada."

Too bad it's Canada?! I stared at the man but no suitable reply came to my mind.

Too bad it's Canada! Wow!

48: Lest we forget. I can't...

We somberly celebrate 'Remembrance Day' thinking of the fallen soldiers who gave their live for peace and freedom during WWI and WWII. Countless other wars have taken place since 1945 all over the world, revolutions, conflicts, uprisings and last but not least, the "Cold War" in Europe.

The bone of contention was Germany. It was divided into East and West. The capital city of Berlin was cut up into four zones and was an island in the eastern communist ruled part of Germany. The Russian part of Berlin was encircled by a wall, a wall built over night in 1961. Impenetrable fences and raked mine fields with watch towers manned with sharp shooters every few hundred meters were around the borders of East Germany, known as the German Democratic Republic. The wall in Berlin and the death zones around the borders were not built to keep terrorists 'out' but to keep the citizens 'in'. Thousands of people risked their lives to escape. There was a first uprising in East Germany in 1953. It was brutally suppressed. Russian tanks moved in and fired warning shots into the air, teargas and water cannons broke up the demonstrators. I escaped in 1955. I can still hear the shots fired after me but I was lucky. Very lucky. My second sister escaped in 1956. My parents had waited for their youngest daughter to graduate. They tried it on the 12th of August 1961. Father had a kidney attack on the way to the station and was taken to the hospital. My mother and my youngest sister went back home. Thank goodness they had not thrown away the key. The next day a wall was up around East Berlin, the only place where it still had been possible to get out. For my parents and my youngest sister the dream of freedom was over.

My father died in 1983. Had he lived to 1989 tears would have run down his cheeks. Hundreds of thousands of demonstrators and protesters were on the streets in East Berlin in 1989. The peaceful demonstrations, growing in size every day went on for weeks requesting freedom of speech, freedom to travel, and democracy. Reactions from the leaders were not encouraging but without a direct order from Moscow the East German government couldn't do anything as drastic as in 1953. People were shaking in their boots but kept joining the demonstrators. Politicians on both sides of the two Germanys were afraid the protests would lead to WW III. Would the Russians move in with their tanks? Everybody expected it at any moment.

Let me share an account of Andreas Macke, a young soldier stationed in West Germany at the time:

"By late October 1989, things had reached an amazing level of tension and anxiety. Looking on from the West, we were feeling pretty damn helpless. And then, in early November, it was as if the East German regime just gave up. No shots were fired.

No tanks suppressed the protests. Instead, a couple of border crossings where thousands of protesters had gathered were simply abandoned by the border guards. Many put their guns down and joined the exodus into West Berlin. And just like that, on November 9th 1989 the infamous Berlin Wall "fell". Many people collected pieces of it "for good luck".

Journalists called the fall of the Berlin Wall "the greatest event after the fall of the Roman Empire".

It was mind boggling to witness the festive mood of thousands of people. With any available tools they hacked away at 'The Wall'. Champagne was flowing, freedom songs were sung, people were dancing on the wall! No tanks, no shooting, no teargas, no water cannons. The guards had just put down their guns and watched. My father had predicted it years before it happened. What nobody, absolutely nobody could have imagined, had happened. The Cold War had ended - WW III had been avoided.

For now.

The shots fired in Ottawa/Canada on October 26th 2014 were a wake-up call. It brought the fear of war closer to home. The Russian invasion of Crimea, the ongoing fighting in the Middle East, the West's involvement in Iraq, the mass migrations of people fleeing their countries, all these do not forebode well.

Let's be alert. Let's remember.

"Lest we forget".

49: What if...

Where is YOUR paradise? Try imagery. In a relaxation class
we learn to imagine a beautiful place, let our thoughts fly there,
feel the sunshine, see the flowers, hear the crashing waves of the
ocean or the wind rustling in big trees. Where are your thoughts
going? Mine always go to the Hawaiian Islands. Hawaii offers all
facets of beauty. It's a feast for the eyes, the scent of the flowers
please the nose, freshly cut pineapples make the mouth water and
the warm sand under bare feet and the sun on my back make me
feel happy. But it is the serenity, tranquility and the sense of the
"Aloha" which encompasses all of this in its people in the parts
of the Islands still truly "Hawaiian". To find the "Aloha" don't go
where the action is: seek out the quiet areas. On the Big Island
night lights along the roads are not allowed. Once I was under a
black velvet night sky with trillions of diamond stars so close
over my head I thought I could touch them. It was so endlessly
dark and sparkling but it was the unearthly stillness which got to
me. I wanted to kneel down and melt and become part of it all.

Does this make sense? It's hard to explain. I went back to the
same spot on the Big Island several years in a row but I have
never seen the sky so near and never had this almost out of body
experience again. It left a longing in me and I wonder if it will
ever be fulfilled. Did you ever say to someone "Can you *hear*
how still it is?"

I love old movies. Purely by coincidence I happened to come
across the movie "From here to Eternity". A happy lighthearted
soldiers' tale – until - did you guess it? No, I don't think so. We
don't talk about that anymore. Until the Japanese fighter aircraft
appeared like a swarm of hornets and disrupted breakfast on a
Sunday morning with many of the navy personnel not even

awake or still in underpants. The scenes of the filming brought back memories of my first visit to Pearl Harbour many years ago. Taken totally by surprise thousands of young men were killed by an attack from a country with whom the US was not even at war. The US Naval ships docked in Pearl Harbour were destroyed on that fateful Sunday, December 7th 1941. The USA, who diplomatically had tried not to get involved in WWII was drawn into it. The rest is history.

Writing my memories of WWII down in the book "We Don't Talk About That" published in 2014 my friends always comment what a relief it must have been for me to "get it all off my chest". I must admit the opposite has happened. I have never thought about it as much as I do now. I have never been more interested in war history as I am now. The more I think and read and follow the news and see the larger picture, the more I see many seemingly small incidents having had large consequences. It's almost like a network of roots branching out in every direction. I can't help asking myself what would have happened if …the Versailles Treaty had been more fair… what if the Art Academy in Vienna would have accepted Hitler as a student, what if one of the many assassination attempts on Hitler's life had succeeded…what if Hitler had not invaded Russia… what if he had not fought on so many fronts…what if the US had not entered the war…what if so many of the old honorable generals from WWI had not been murdered and what if Field Marshal Rommel had not been ordered to commit suicide… what if the Jews who had lived in Germany for hundreds of years were not killed or driven out of Germany… what if they had remained part of the German people? I have so many more 'ifs'. How would our world look today?

Would it be the paradise we imagined in our relaxation class?

192

50: The Weeping Angel

Big tears were welling up behind his eyelids. He tried very hard to blink them away. He was flying within a large flock of fellow angels - wings spread wide, arms outstretched as if ready to embrace the whole world. You see, this angel was new at angel-ling. He could not yet hide his feelings behind an angelic smile.

He couldn't take his eyes off the planet Earth: There it was, hanging in the atmosphere, slowly, ever so slowly, turning around and around. Because of this, our angel could see many different countries, many different people, and all were doing many different things. It was Christmas time, the time when humans on Earth celebrate the Lord Jesus' birth. They did so in different ways in different countries, even on different dates. They do so every year, have done so for more than two-thousand years. Now, once again, they were singing of love and 'Peace on Earth'. They were giving presents to each other and thinking more than usually of sharing with the less fortunate and helping the poor. Our angel wondered: Why didn't they do this all year 'round? Didn't the Lord say, "The left hand does not need to know what the right one does"? Does it not mean they don't need a reason for helping in such a generous way once a year? Why wait for Christmas? Couldn't it be like Christmas all year round?

Oh, our angel thought, there is so much trouble down there. The humans are trying to destroy each other and their beautiful blue planet in the process.

It was not the fire from the deep bowels of the Earth, spat out by angry boiling volcanoes, which was trying to reach way up into the sky. It was not the tournedos wreaking havoc. It was not the rivers swelling up and flooding entire villages. And it was not the forest fires lit by electrical storms or stupid human mistakes such as throwing away glass or plastic bottles which intensified the sun's rays, or cigarette butts carelessly flipped away. No. No, it was fire made by the humans to destroy other humans, burn each other's cities and kill each other's people. They call it "War." There seems to be war in many countries, on many continents. Were neighbours killing neighbours? It seemed to be so. There were thousands leaving their homes and all they owned behind. Our angel spotted a prison camp in the middle of nowhere. You couldn't escape from there. A high barbed wire fence was built around it anyway. Watch-towers were on the four corners, and several heavily clad soldiers on each tower with machine guns pointed to a group of shivering men in the middle of a square. Many had no shoes, just old rags wrapped around frostbitten feet. A warmly-dressed commander stood before them. A huge flag on the pole beside him did not move. It was twilight, the time between the parting day and the rapidly approaching night. Frost crackled in the air. The breath of the men, coming like tiny puffs of smoke, suspended over and around each of them. What an eerie scene, useless in the big picture of history, but already part of it.

Wait! What was that? Sounds of music? Was that a sound coming from a single, shy voice in the wintry night air? The sound got louder, stronger, steadier as all the men in the middle of the square joined in, despite the warning shots fired, bouncing off the hard, frozen earth. Loud and clear it rang up to the sky:

"Silent night, holy night, all is calm, all is bright..."

The flock of angels slowed their flight, even descended a little. They were allowed to do that if they saw something unusual, you know. A magical night it was. A wondrous feeling was evoked by this chorus of men in the middle of nowhere, kept in a camp from which there was no escape, even if the barbed wire fence and the guns were not in place. The angel saw the men felt lost but they had hope against hope.

Is there still a chance for "Peace on Earth"? Maybe. Maybe all isn't lost yet, thought our angel. But look, what is happening? All the armed soldiers put down their guns. They joined the singing in a strange, guttural language. As our flock of angels moved on they saw and heard it happen in many countries as they passed over the slowly, ever so slowly turning planet Earth. Soldiers came out of the trenches and shook hands with their enemy, even gave each other little gifts and kicked a soccer ball around. Tomorrow is another day; they will have to obey orders and shoot at each other again.

The tears behind our angel's eyelids welled up mightily. No blinking them away anymore. Large and hot, they silently rolled over his cheeks and dripped down into the frosty air below. They froze to tiny icicles, falling, falling and falling until they reached warmer air, melted slightly, changed their shape and turned into snowflakes. They drifted down to planet Earth, a few at first, then more and more, and still more! You see, all the angels had started weeping, just as all the men had joined the singing in all those languages. It only took one to take courage and start the song. The angels flapped their wings to keep themselves steady in the air. Because of all the flapping, a wind came up.

The wind made the snowflakes dance, up and down, around and around. Soon the air was filled with snowflakes, closer and closer to planet Earth they drifted. They fell on the upturned faces of the singing men, they fell on people who were lost; they fell on children who had nothing to eat or didn't even have a place to call home. The snowflakes mingled with all their tears. Soon you wouldn't know which of the drops, rolling down young and old cheeks, were tears and which the melting snowflakes. The cold dark night, the endless loneliness of a faraway but star filled sky filled the hearts of all people with a longing so strong it hurt. How they all wanted to be with their loved ones, oh, to have a bed again, a warm room, a warm coat, and hot soup to fill the stomach. But mostly, they were longing for 'Peace on Earth'.

And so it was, and so it is: When you see a single snow flake drift down, look up for others. Because, angels fly in flocks you see, and when one is sad and sheds a tear, it is never over a trivial thing. Therefore, all the other angels will be kind and supportive and compassionate, and soon, very soon, they cry too. During all the commotion, they will lose height and will have to flap their wings, just like birds, to stay in the air. And the flapping causes a wind to come up and the wind makes the snowflakes dance. You can count on it. The angels are just overhead.

You don't believe me? Go out on a snowy winter night at Christmas. You will see it for yourself.

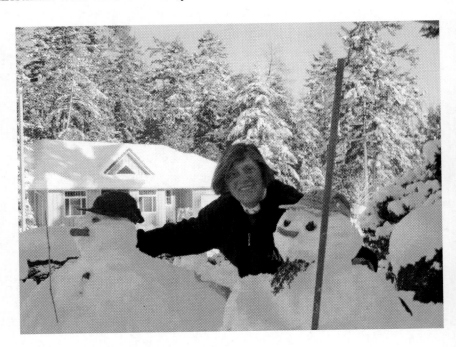

Other books by Giselle Roeder

Healing with Water – Kneipp Therapy at Home- 2000
"The author, health writer and teacher Giselle Roeder trained extensively in Kneipp Therapy in her native Germany. Here she combines personal anecdotes and a thorough understanding of her subject to deliver a simple message in a highly useable and inspiring format."

Sauna – The Hottest Way to Good Health – 2001
"Roeder's uplifting common-sense style and many enticing photographs support the book's instructions. A final section filled with tantalizing, elegantly present recipes is a perfect complement to the therapeutic sauna lifestyle. Cleansing and detoxifying juices, colourful fresh salads and soups are the work of highly acclaimed natural chef Fred Edrissi."

We Don't Talk About That – An Amazing Story of Survival – 2014
"I found this book to be a compelling read. This is a very timely memoir. Read it."
"Giselle Roeder's book is gripping and poignant. She engages the reader, leading them gently by the hand, on a whirlwind journey back through time to relive the events before, during and after the WW2 that have shaped the lives of millions."
"Finally I purchased your book. I started reading and couldn't put it down. It isn't just good it is very good."
"If it were not so harrowing, it should be desired reading in schools & given the same historical literary importance as 'The Diary of Anne Frank'."

Coming in 2016: Sequel to **We Don't Talk About That** working title:
Bridging Two Continents – A Roller Coaster Ride Over Three Decades